The Hidden Years

PHILBY
The Hidden Years

Morris Riley

JANUS PUBLISHING COMPANY
London, England

First published by United Writers Publications Ltd
Penzance, England

ISBN 1 85200 029 5

First paperback edition published in Great Britain 1999
by Janus Publishing Company Limited,
Edinburgh House, 19 Nassau Street,
London W1N 7RE

www.januspublishing.co.uk

A catalogue record for this book
is available from the British Library.

ISBN 1 85756 344 1

Phototypeset in 11 on 13.5 Sabon
by Keyboard Services, Luton, Beds

Cover design Creative Line

Printed and bound in Great Britain by
Athenæum Press Limited, Gateshead, Tyne & Wear

With special thanks to RA and JR

With special thanks to R.S. and J.L.

CONTENTS

ACKNOWLEDGEMENTS

The author wishes to thank the following people for specific help in his research for this book:

General Clyde Rich (US), Colonels Neil McLean, James Johnson, David Smiley, David Stirling and Edgar O'Ballance; Commanders Donald McCormick and Anthony Courtney; Dr W. Mann, Wilbur Crane Eveland, Kermit Roosevelt, James Jesus Angleton, Miles Copeland, Hillair du Berrier, P. F. De Villemarest, The Duc de Grantmesnil, Teddy Kollek, Brian Freemantle, Phillip Knightley, Richard Winch, John E. Taylor, Lauren Paine, Ray Alan, Montague Woodhouse, Peter Wright, Diana de Vries, George Miller, Keith Bush, June Cook, Anthony Verrier, Colin Legum, R. J. Fletcher, Anthony Cavendish, George Kennedy Young, Verne E. Newton, Julian Amery, Chapman Pincher, the (former) Sultan of Lahej, and Prince Yahyia al-Hirsi.

Permission to quote extracts from the following sources is also gratefully acknowledged:

Philby, KGB Masterspy by Phillip Knightley, published by Andre Deutch Ltd in 1988.

The Belarus Secret by John Loftus, edited by Nathan Miller, published by Penguin Books in 1983.

My Silent War by Kim Philby, published by Grafton Books, a division of the Collins Publishing Group.

The Philby Affair by Hugh Trevor-Roper, published by Thorsons, a division of the Collins Publishing Group.

Nightwatch published by the Security and Intelligence Foundation, Arlington, Vancouver, USA.

The Lobster, No. 16, published by Stephen Dorril and Robin Ramsey.

The KGB by Harry Rositke, published by Sidgwick & Jackson Ltd.

The Climate Of Treason by Andrew Boyle, published by Century Hutchinson Publishing Group Ltd.

The quote from Ray Alan's article reprinted with permission of *The New Leader*, June 25, 1984. Copyright © the American Labor Conference on International Affairs, Inc.

PUBLISHER'S NOTE

Philby: The Hidden Years was first published in 1990. It had not been submitted either to the D-Notice Committee, nor the Secret Intelligence Service (SIS) for vetting. On the first day of publication the publisher, Malcolm Sheppard, United Writers Publications received threatening telephone calls over publication – so much so that he became ill. Four days later a former SIS agent, a journalist, threatened the publisher by telephone with legal action. Publication was withdrawn. Sheppard was subsequently advised by James Rusbridger, another SIS agent, that 'Had [the SIS agent, deleted] not taken action, someone else would have done on behalf to SIS'.

Three months later, Morris Riley was advised by a former SIS officer as to what needed to be checked by the censor, and that has been done in this edition. This is shown in the form of the areas questioned, now passed by lawyers, being underlined. All passages censored have been done so on the grounds of national security and the Official Secret Act(s).

PREFACE

The differences between what was originally published in the 1990 edition in terms of what has been deleted from the present edition are very interesting indeed.

After submitting the proof edition to Rear Rdmiral D. M. Pulvertaft of the Defence, Press and Broadcasting Advisory Committee, he replied, in part:

> As the 1990 edition was not forwarded to this office I cannot say whether my predecessors would have asked for any changes but I can assure you that the SIS have no knowledge of any attempt to put pressure on you or your publisher as is suggested in the Publisher's Note on page x of the proof. I suspect that, if such pressures were exerted, it was as a result of rivalry within the intelligence writer's fraternity or an individual threatening some sort of legal action.

He was, of course, totally correct about 'an individual threatening some sort of legal action' on the day of publication as a matter of fact. Advance copies had been sent only to former security and intelligencce officers and agents and not to the media. The fact was that the former SIS agent, CENSORED, had done so on behalf of SIS. Lest it be thought otherwise, a certain Colonel had informed me two weeks before publication that he had been approached by SIS in the event that, from a legal point of view, he could stop publication of the book.

In the event, the decent and most honourable Colonel did not do so.

The publisher received various threatening telephone calls, one purporting to be from the Press Council wanting the names of CENSORED and CENSORED deleted – hardly the wishes of the 'rivalry within the intelligence writer's fraternity'.

Lastly after publication a well-advised former SIS officer demanded that:

> It is ESSENTIAL to OMIT the following: (1) Footnote 37 (2) The last sentence (After all ... officers). You cannot accuse someone of murder...

(He also demanded the deletion of the name of an SIS employed individual who acted in a most treacherous manner during the Suez operation which endangered the lives of British military personnel.) His name has been deleted from this edition.

Recently, after decades of silence, alleged assassination attempts became the flavour ot the month. In August 1998 the former Security Service officer, David Shayler, stated that he would publish on the Internet that SIS had been involved in assassination plots against foreign targets, including an attempt to blow up Colonel Muammer Gadaffi, the Libyan dictator. Should this have been the case, it would have been the first known case since planned but aborted attempts to kill President Nasser in the mid-1950s. See page 83 of this book.

INTRODUCTION

The last major book about H. A. R. 'Kim' Philby was published in 1988. So, why another book concerning one of Britain's major Soviet agents, you may ask? Is his story not stale, and what is so new about the man who died only two years ago?

First of all, one must explain that this book is not yet another biography about Philby. Instead, it concentrates on the operations he was involved in for the British Secret Intelligence Service (SIS) and the Russian Intelligence Service (RIS).

This book begins when Philby joined the Service in 1940 (for readers who want to learn about his early life, they are referred to other main books about Philby listed in the notes). Not only do the early chapters provide a comprehensive coverage of the time when he was an officer between 1940 and 1951, they cover such unpublished areas as Philby and Spain when it is alleged that he had an unkindly hand in the fate of certain Anarchists, but was a chief recruiter, in a major operation, of former Nazi war criminals, some of whom came to Britain.

The Hidden Years shows for the first time that Philby has been far more dangerous than previously supposed: the impact he had on the shaping of British Middle East policy in the 1940s, '50s and '60s, and on certain Soviet foreign security affairs since he defected in 1963.

Prior to his exposure in Washington in 1951, Philby had

caused the deaths of countless agents not only in the publicized case of Albania, but also throughout the Eastern bloc. Many people are under the false impression that following his exposure (and subsequent flight in 1963) Philby was no longer effective or active. The reality, as this book shows, is somewhat different, because he did far more damage after 1951 to British-American Security relations, and work of a very high value for the RIS, than he ever achieved while his cover was still secure. Not only was Philby employed by Britain and Russia* but he was also an agent for the CIA, which he helped to form.

The 'core' of this book explores the 'Hidden Years' of 1956 to 1963, virtually ignored by all other writers. In the 1950s the Middle East had become a theatre of conflict between East and West. We examine the countries involved, Egypt, Syria, Iraq and Lebanon in terms of how the conflict arose; the subsequent wars between the East and the West, and the contribution of Philby – in whom the Soviets had a ruthless ally.

In his early days, Philby had recruited many people. In the Near East, he influenced, for example, the output of propaganda media, controlled by SIS and financed by the British Treasury, that pushed anti-American propaganda and material hostile to British interests in the region.

This book, for the first time, explores the deadly collaboration between Philby and another highly-placed Soviet agent, George Blake, which led to the deaths of Allied agents in the

---

* The terms 'double' or 'treble agent' (much loved, but incorrectly employed by the media) have not been employed as Philby never was either. 'Originally', as explained by a former CIA officer, 'a double agent was a spy who enjoyed such confidence of both sides that he knew the secrets of both, and could report them back and forth as he wished. Once Kim Philby became a Soviet agent, the Soviets saw to it that from that moment on he had no access to Soviet secrets. Philby was in no sense a double agent: he was a British security officer, but he was an agent only to the Soviets. It was only to the Soviet side that he had the one essential quality of the agent: access to the target.'

Ukraine. In addition, it reveals how Blake was converted to Marxism by a British official, and was blackmailed into becoming an RIS agent.

We also see Philby's last role for the RIS in the Middle East in the pre-coup period to the revolution in North Yemen in September 1962. After the coup, partly in response to the involvement of Philby, the British government launched an arms-length highly clandestine mercenary operation involving members of the Special Air Service (SAS) and SIS, which was sanctioned by the Prime Minister. This operation is examined in depth.

After Philby defected to the Soviet Union in 1963, we discover how he rose in the ranks of the RIS to General. His last and largest role began in 1971 when he became head of the Department of Western Propaganda, part of Novosti. It was now that he caused a big blow against SIS, when in two published articles, he totally 'blew' operations in the Middle East, and the identities of minor and major SIS officers and agents (some of the officers have reached high positions of office since then). Lastly, we see how even over the last five years, in his pivotal position both within Novosti and the KGB, Philby had given his advice over Soviet involvement and the peace movements in Europe; and according to a former Vice-Chief of SIS, was occasionally brought to Moscow by the RIS 'to confront and embarrass American visitors who have had former CIA connections'.

It was not until 1982 that I began to take an interest in Philby while engaged in research on the Middle East. I discovered that he had been involved in a little-known coup in North Yemen.

Soon afterwards I met George Miller, at that time a research officer at the Institute for European Defence and Strategic Studies, who explained how both Philby and Blake had worked together in the mid-1950s (unpublished) and had caused the deaths of Allied agents, in the Soviet Union.

My interest in Philby was then fully aroused and I read the major books about him. It soon became obvious that the books contained a considerable amount of background information, but very little about what he actually did in terms of his betrayals and the recruitment of agents (and 'agents of influence') for the USSR, and the operations he was involved in.

I, therefore, concentrated on these areas, and discovered a considerable amount of new unpublished material(s) which I placed in a file entitled 'Philby Operations: East/West' which represents the major part of this book. The penultimate chapter, 'The Philby Jigsaw' looks at his motivation, and pulls together the story of Philby from his early days at Trinity College, Cambridge to his defection in January 1963.

Morris Riley, May 1989

1999 UPDATE

During the 1980s very little was published about Philby. One exception was *Philby, KGB Masterspy* by Phillip Knightley. Since 1990, however, there have been over a dozen articles and three books. To now include all of the new relevant information would mean rewriting all of the 1990 edition. Instead, I have reviewed the books, now included after the appendix.

Morris Riley, January 1999

1

THE NEW RECRUIT

In the summer of 1940 'Kim' Philby entered what was to become the pinnacle of his early career on behalf of the USSR – the penetration of SIS.

Prior to 1940, whilst in Nazi Germany, and later in Spain where he acted as a correspondent for *The Times*, Philby had 'half expected' an approach from 'a British intelligence representative':

> I was confident that I would recognise my man the moment he made his first cautious soundings. He would be lean, and bronzed, of course, with a clipped moustache, clipped accent and, most probably, a clipped mind. He would ask me to stick my neck out for country and frown austerely if I mentioned pay.[1]

Alas, however, this was not to occur. But in June 1940, events were about to take a welcome turn for Philby, who was now back in England, having been evacuated twice from Brest and from Boulogne. He was still a correspondent for *The Times*, but was increasingly disenchanted with his role owing to Army field censorship which had killed his interest in being a war correspondent. 'Try writing a war report without mentioning a single place-name or designating a single unit and you will see what I mean.'[2] Even when back in England, Philby was not at all pleased with the articles he produced; he considered them 'dreadful rubbish', and he felt that he was generally at a 'loose end'.

Philby decided to leave *The Times* but did not want to be conscripted into the army. Therefore, he applied for a vacancy with the Government Code Cypher School – an establishment which cracked enemy and friendly countries codes. He thought he had a 'promising interview' with Frank Birch, a leading light at the School, who before and after the war was a Don at King's College, Cambridge. However, Birch eventually rejected Philby on the grounds that he could not offer him enough in the way of financial remuneration. Philby then found himself going to Holloway for an army medical examination.

Guy Burgess, another part of the infamous Philby Circle, who had acted as a financial conduit to Philby when Philby had spied on Franco, had been manoeuvring on Philby's behalf within Section D. The 'D' was an abbreviation for destruction, and was set up by Colonel Laurence Grand in 1938. Burgess 'was forever vaunting the intellectual and moral gifts of his friends [and] thereupon recommended Kim'.[3] Eventually, Ralph Deakin, the then Foreign Editor of *The Times*, received a telephone call from the War Office, inquiring as to whether Philby was 'available for war work'.[4] The call, and approach, according to Philby, and confirmed by authors Bruce Page, David Leitch and Phillip Knightley, was made by Captain Leslie Sheridan. (In 1938, Sheridan, then a *Daily Mirror* Night Editor, joined the newly formed D-Section in order to organize its press operation against Nazi Germany.) Before Sheridan's phone call, Philby had applied 'on Burgess's advice',[5] for a vacancy within Section D. Subsequently, Philby received a telephone call from the War Office suggesting a meeting which was to be held in the foyer of a small hotel, the St Ermin's in Caxton Street. Upon his arrival, he found himself being appraised by a very shrewd, middle-aged spinster called Miss Marjorie Maxse who was a War Office intermediary. Philby 'acquitted himself to Miss Maxse's satisfaction',[6] especially in relation to ideas on the subversion of

Nazi Germany. As they parted, Maxse asked Philby to meet her again a few days later at the same hotel. This he did, but this time Maxse was accompanied by Guy Burgess who had volunteered his presence in order to confirm, contest, or reject, the initial impression gained by Maxse as to Philby's suitability.

> I was put through my paces again. Encouraged by Guy's presence I began to show off, name-dropping shamelessly as one does at interviews. From time to time my interlocutors exchanged glances; Guy would nod gravely and approvingly. It turned out I was wasting my time as a decision had already been taken. Before we parted, Miss Maxse informed me that, if I agreed, I should sever my connection with *The Times* and report for duty to Guy Burgess at an address in Caxton Street, in the same block as the St Ermin's Hotel ... I decided that it was my duty to profit from the experience of the only secret service man of my acquaintance. So I spent the weekend drinking with Guy Burgess. On the following Monday, I reported to him formally. We both had slight headaches.[7]

Had a competent security check been made – in those days positive vetting had never been heard of – Philby would soon have been labelled either a Communist or a Nazi, indeed at different times perhaps even both. As it was, his new employers made a routine reference to the Security Service, MI5, and according to Philby received the laconic statement that nothing was recorded against him. He was duly hired by David Footman. Philby found himself working for the Secret Intelligence Service (SIS) which was responsible for and in charge of all secret intelligence work, both espionage and counter-espionage, on non-British soil. At that time there was intense rivalry in terms of geographical spheres between SIS and the other major arm of British Security, the Security Service. This rivalry was about which organization was in charge of all the counter-espionage and security in Britain as well as all British overseas colonies. At the beginning of World War II both services still carried the flavour of Buchan and Kipling in the form of tight-lipped military men who were somehow stamped in the mould of

Buchan's Brigadier-General Hannay. One applicant, Bickham Sweet-Escott, caught the flavour of this military caste when confronted in a bare War Office room by an officer in civilian clothes: 'I can't tell you what sort of job it would be. All I can say is that if you join us, you mustn't be afraid of forgery, and you mustn't be afraid of murder.'[8]

It was into this enclave that Burgess introduced Philby and where they both worked for Section D. Section D acted as an underground intelligence-gathering organization in foreign countries, and also conducted what E. H. Cookridge described as 'irregular warfare'. Prior to the outbreak of World War II, 'a number of brilliant men from industry and the universities had joined Colonel Grand and his Chief of Staff, Major George Taylor, a tough Australian'.[9] A Central Register contained the names of the volunteers who had specialized knowledge of Europe and in addition, at various times, must have rendered service to SIS. Furthermore, each had agreed to rejoin in the event of war. Such well-known entrants included George Cour-tauld, of Courtauld Ltd; Sir Francis Glyn of the banking house of Glyn Mills and Co; Charles des Graz, Chairman of Sothebys; 'Bill' Stephenson, the Canadian millionaire; barristers such as George Pollock and Leslie Sheridan; the American millionaire Chester A. Beatty; Bickham Sweet-Escott; Oliver Baldwin, son of the former Prime Minister; Freya Stark, the well-known Arabist and writer; as well as journalists and writers, such as Hugh Greene, who became Director General of the BBC in 1960, his brother Graham Greene, H. Montgomery Hyde and Malcolm Muggeridge.

Section D planned various daring operations, including blow-ing up the port installations at Oxelösund and Nyköping in neutral Sweden, from where the Germans were shipping iron ore. The sabotage plan had to be abandoned because the Swedish authorities heard a rumour of a conspiracy by British agents. From time to time they achieved success. As German troops were occupying the Netherlands, Lieutenant-Colonel M. R. Chidson made a weekend dash to Amsterdam and returned with industrial diamonds worth £1¼ million. In June 1940, Norman Hope rescued Madam de Gaulle from France.[10]

Since the SIS did not want attention brought to its units operating in Europe, they viewed the proposed acts of sabotage, masterminded by Colonel Grand, with positive disfavour. As a result, Section D was starved of funds and personnel and had to reappraise its role.

Within a few days of starting in Section D, Philby met Grand whom he described as follows: 'his mind was certainly not clipped. It ranged free and handsome over the whole field of his awesome responsibilities, never shrinking from any idea, however big or wild.'

In July Burgess met Philby in his office and he showed 'Kim' a memorandum which he had written; it had been approved of generally by Colonel Grand who had asked for a further study and elaboration of the subject. Burgess proposed the establishment of a school for training agents in the techniques of underground work – quite an astonishing proposal as it had never been made before and no similar school existed. But he required Philby's help in improving the proposals. In due course, Brickendonbury Hall, a former school building standing in spacious grounds near Hertford, was acquired for training purposes. The duo then travelled to Brickendonbury Hall, and were introduced to a Commander R. N. Peters who had been seconded to act as School Commandant. Much to Philby's surprise, Peters appeared to: 'against all the odds ... took an immediate fancy [liking] to Guy.' Peters also repeatedly took the duo to his favourite restaurant in Soho, The Hungaria.

The training staff at the Hall was soon increased by the influx of foreign propaganda specialists and explosives experts. The most outstanding personality in Philby's opinion was an art-dealer of great distinction called Tommy Harris who was employed 'as a sort of glorified house-keeper, largely because he and his wife were inspired cooks'. SIS at Caxton Street also sent down a batch of twenty-five Norwegian, Belgian and Spanish pupils who were all to be groomed as saboteurs. For good measure a few trainers were also tossed in, but Philby was doubtful as to whether the trainees picked up any useful tips. As the summer months passed without any clear directives from London, Commander Peters tired of the whole episode and resigned. Burgess, whilst in London, discovered that Section D was to be brutally dismembered. As a result, SIS lost the section, and now a new organization called the Special Operations Executive (SOE) was created by Cabinet directive, 22 July, 1940.[11] It emerged as a Section D clone.

The instigator of this reorganization was Prime Minister Churchill who had asked Dr Hugh Dalton – the Minister of Economic Warfare – to deal with the replanning of the insufficient and diverse units within the orbit of planning sabotage and propaganda. According to Dalton:

> This was an instrument of war and I should be responsible for shaping it. I accepted the Prime Minister's invitation with great eagerness and satisfaction. 'And now,' Churchill exhorted me, 'set Europe ablaze.'[12]

INSIDE SOE

After the reorganization, Philby and Burgess reported to the new HQ of Special Operations based at 64 Baker Street, London. Now SOE was divided into two branches: SO1 which was concerned with black propaganda and subsequently renamed the Political Warfare Executive, and SO2, the Section D clone dealing with subversion and sabotage. Philby found himself for a period being paid £50 per month, without any trouble from the Inland Revenue, but not doing any work. Eventually, Major-General Colin Gubbins, who had been put in charge of a training programme, summoned Philby and asked if he knew anything about propaganda. Philby replied in the affirmative. Gubbins then explained that a new training establishment was being planned on an ambitious scale containing technical schools for demolition and wireless communication. In addition, Gubbins was introducing a central school for general training in the arts of subversion and sabotage – and because underground propaganda was one of the arts required, he was looking for a suitable instructor. Philby was requested to go away and produce a draft on the subject outlining a clear propaganda training syllabus. Gubbins thereupon showed Philby to the door with the words: 'Make it short'. This Philby did, with assistance, into a page and a half of foolscap, and then telephoned Gubbins to say that it was ready. Within five minutes Gubbins was back on the line to Philby, explaining that he had arranged a meeting in Charles Hambro's office that afternoon to discuss the paper. According to Philby:

> Gubbins brought several of his staff officers along to the meeting. Hambro greeted us in his friendly, comfortable way, making us all feel at home. He took my paper and read it aloud, slowly and deliberately. At the end of it, he remarked that it all sounded very sensible. Gubbins's officers nodded in brisk no-nonsense manner; they looked intensely military. To my surprise, Gubbins was smiling happily. 'Exactly what I wanted,' he said emphatically. 'Exactly ... what do you say, Charles?' Hambro said nothing in particular. 'Go ahead and do just that,' Gubbins told me. The meeting was over.[13]

Philby then moved to a desk in Gubbins's offices, and not at 64 Baker Street. His new location was up Baker Street going towards Regent's Park, and it was there he expanded his draft syllabus into a complete series of full lectures. The new school was established in Beaulieu, Hampshire, and although of an amateurish nature it was a distinct improvement compared to Brickendonbury Hall. It was to these pleasant surroundings that Philby was posted; the school inhabited several country houses on the Montague estate at Beaulieu. Agents who had completed commando and parachute training arrived for a three-week course in such topics as: 'the recognition of enemy troops, police forces and officials; the use of codes, passwords and secret messages; how to keep alive in enemy-held territory; and finally the art of clandestine propaganda – a field in which Kim, on slender evidence, was considered an expert.'[14] The several country houses contained many people of different nationalities all undergoing training for subsequent employment in their German-occupied homelands. Philby also took the course himself but never went to Europe. Instead he became an instructor. Ironically enough, Philby had to warn some trainees, primarily from Poland, Scandinavia, and a few from the Balkans – all of whom had no love for the Russians – that it was their mission not to blow up Russians, but to blow up the Germans first. He also specialized in printing; in fact, there was a scheme for suborning linotype operators in German-occupied countries, and trips were arranged for trainees to visit *The Times* office in London to familiarize trainees with printing machinery.

Philby was admired by his pupils, and his SOE seniors were impressed by his reputation gained while being a war correspondent. Had he possessed negative traits, then he would not have risen as far as he did in SIS, and would certainly have been a disappointment to the USSR. In fact, since the late thirties, Philby's main ambition had been to join and penetrate British intelligence. No doubt, when he joined Colonel Grand's Section D in mid-1940, he thought that he had made it. But Brickendonbury Hall and the SOE training establishment at Beaulieu hardly provided him with access to classified information and the promotion ladder required by the Soviets. To accomplish this aim, he looked for access into mainstream SIS work.

Once more, access came about through a friend, in the form of Tommy Harris. He and Philby often met at Harris's home at Chesterfield Gardens, London, in the evenings, with several other friends. Food and wine flowed at the meetings; indeed, at all other hours of the day and night. The Harris household 'became an off-duty meeting place for a small group of men from MI5 and MI6 [SIS]'[15] who formed a group called 'the Outfit'. The most senior member was Dick Brooman-White, head of SIS's Iberian Section, Harris's boss. During one visit to Chesterfield Gardens Harris asked Philby if he would be interested in a job that called for some of his special knowledge of Spain's espionage, for the purpose of obtaining advance information of operations mounted against British territory from the Iberian Peninsula. (Section Five specialized in obtaining such information from 'neutral' territories.) According to Harris, Section Five was not providing an adequate service. And a high proportion of German intelligence operations targeted against Britain were being mounted from the Iberian Peninsula. The sub-section dealing with Spain and Portugal was to be expanded, including an expansion from two to six officers. Harris thought that Philby's name could be put forward should he be interested. Philby, of course, was certainly interested, and he told Harris that he wanted 'to think it over'. A few days later, he told Harris that he 'would be most grateful if he [Harris] took the matter further'.

Wheels were now set in motion with Harris proposing Philby to Brooman-White, who in turn recommended him to Colonel Felix Cowgill, the head of Section Five. In addition to the approval of Cowgill, some form of vetting was required by Colonel Valentine Vivian, the Deputy Chief of SIS. Subsequently vetting took the form of a luncheon meeting between Vivian, Philby and his father, Sir John Philby. (The latter was known to Vivian as they were both in India prior to World War I.)

When Kim went out to the lavatory, I asked Sir John about him. 'He was a bit of a Communist at Cambridge, wasn't he?' I enquired. 'Oh, that was all schoolboy nonsense,' Sir John replied. 'He's a reformed character now.'[16]

Once again, everything worked well for Philby, and he found himself heading for Section Five which was based near to St Albans, within commuting distance of London. His arrival was eagerly awaited – according to the famous historian, Hugh Trevor-Roper:

As an undergraduate at Oxford I had heard admiring accounts of him from a friend [Tim Milne – but never named in this account]. And, sure enough, while we [Section Five] were waiting for Philby, my old Oxford friend himself [Milne] appeared in Section Five as a herald of the coming Messiah.[17]

2

THE COMING MESSIAH

When Philby arrived at Section Five, he found himself in a new world of counter-espionage which had a dual function within SIS. Half of the SIS organization in London ran intelligence gathering stations on foreign soil known as 'G' Sections; the other half, known as 'Circulating Stations', processed information received from the 'G' Sections. The information was then passed on to relevant government departments. 'G' Sections were organized on a country or regional basis, whereas the Circulating Sections were organized with reference to subject matter. Both Sections were then divided under Army, Navy and Air Force Sections, as well as a Political Section and an Economic Section. Section Five dealt with counter-espionage, having the tripartite function of collection, evaluation, and action. According to Philby:

> It was responsible for the collection of counter-espionage information from foreign countries by illegal means.[1]

Such illegal means involved bribery, corruption and blackmail of people who had access to relevant information which was needed by SIS field agents. Primarily, they were to work against the German spy networks and, as is still practised by the Security Service and SIS 'watching communications, checking

11

for leaks, analysing the histories of people who hold vital information'.[2]

Philby found himself in a sub-section dealing with the Iberian Peninsula, which at that time was of strategic importance because there were fears of Germany overrunning Spain, taking Gibraltar, and thus closing the Mediterranean to the British. Officially Spain was neutral. However, in practice the Spanish government was proved to be pro-German. During the Spanish Civil War, Hitler had sent the Condor Legion to Franco – this had been one of the major deciding factors in Franco's military victory over the ill-armed Republicans who had to contend with a military blockade imposed by the Allies. Hitler had used Spain as a training ground for the newly reconstructed Luftwaffe. German airmen learnt valuable lessons from their combat experience over Spanish cities, and put them to good effect later on in the Battle of Britain and the Blitz.

The political situation in Spain which existed when Philby joined the Iberian Section of SIS, prior to Franco coming to power, showed an increasing dissatisfaction with the course taken by the Spanish Republic after its inception in 1931. The deeply conservative military finally split in July 1936, in a carefully prepared army revolt against the Republican government. Initially, General Franco was not the leader of the army revolt, but took over its direction after the actual commander was killed in an air crash. Resistance to the revolt became widespread. But neither side – Republican or Nationalist – could achieve a decisive military victory until finally in 1939, when Franco's forces succeeded. The fight against Fascism unleashed deeper passions in areas of Spain which traditionally had strong revolutionary Anarchist or Socialist histories. As the Anarchist writer, Augustin Souchy observed:

When the army and the Fascists rose against the Republic on 19 July 1936, their most vigorous opposition was from the labour move- ment in the big cities, in whose front ranks were the Anarchists and the CNT. They overcame the armed forces and the Fascists in the

12

cities. Owners and executives of big business fled with the army, wealthy landowners abandoned their lands. The workers and their unions lost no time in taking control of the factories and the farms, the railroads, utilities, municipal services, the schools, hospitals, bakeries and dairies. Everything was collectivised. Everything was run by the workers through their unions and factory councils.[3]

Souchy, who had witnessed the collectivization at first hand in Aragon wrote:

> Collectivisation in Spain was the most important transformation in history both of the property structure of the land and the means of production, and the organisation of productive work. The collectives were a realisation of the ideals and theories of free or libertarian socialism, in contrast with the Russian state and even the self-management system in Yugoslavia. The collectives were opposed by the Spanish Communist Party (and Moscow during the Civil War).[4]

The Communist Party, up to the start of the Civil War, had never had much of a following in Spain where historically the Labour movement had preferred the libertarian ideas of the Russian Anarchist, Michael Bakunin, to those of Marx's authoritarian State Socialism. Those attracted to Marxism tended to go towards the Socialists (PSOE) and their union organization the UGT, or to the smaller Trotskyist-influenced Marxist party, the POUM, rather than towards the small and pro-Stalin Communist Party. But with the outbreak of Civil war, the Communists were able to build up firstly through the dual tactics of a massive and well organized infiltration of the Republican army, government machinery, and other, political parties (principally the Socialists) and trade unions. Secondly, the offering of a safe haven for the respectable middle-class who were hostile to the revolutionary experiments of the Anarchists and Socialists but could not openly come out in opposition. As a result of this open-door policy towards the frightened bourgeoisie (and offers of an assisted promotion to army officers who would follow the Comintern line) the membership of the

13

Spanish Communist Party rose dramatically as the Civil War progressed. Comintern policy, decreed by Stalin (who would shortly sign the Hitler-Stalin pact and offer vital military aid and training to the growing Nazi armed forces), was that Spain was not ready for a Socialist revolution, and that Communists should fight to remain a bourgeois republic. Therefore, whilst it was necessary to pay lip-service to the popular revolutionary feeling of the people on the Republican side, in practice it was the duty of all good Communists to stop any serious attempts at Socialist revolution. The biggest obstacle in all this for the Communists was the Anarchists of the FAI and the anarcho-syndicalists of the CNT. The conflict was devastating for the Spanish people. The Communist Party behind the Republican lines, attacked and killed Socialists, Trotskyists, and Anarchists. This particular incident was graphically described by George Orwell in *Homage to Catalonia*. In Barcelona, during the May days of 1937, the CP launched a furious assault on its Anarchist and Trotskyist enemies of the CNT-FAI and the POUM, under the pretext that the Anarchists (who amongst other municipal services controlled the telephone exchange) were tapping the telephone conversations of the government. The purge eventually petered out in a maze of negotiations. But the resulting recriminations and confusion did much to weaken the Republican war effort, and open the way to a Fascist victory.

When Franco and his Fascists won military control over the whole of Spain, those who had fought to defend the Republic disappeared in three directions: prison, exile or clandestinity. Many refused to accept Franco's victory at the end of the war and disappeared into the mountains from which a short-lived guerrilla struggle was fought. Still, others were to wage a longer campaign of resistance from bases in southern France which lasted until the early 1960s. All trade unions became illegal overnight. The main hope amongst the anti-Franco community was that the Allied opposition to Hitler could be extended to include opposition to Franco.

By 1940 the Anarchist organizations in exile – CNT, FAI and

FIJL – regrouped under the banner of the MLE (Spanish Liberation Movement). But it was the MLE which then, almost alone, carried on serious armed resistance to Franco. This fact was not lost on SIS, who knew also that Spanish Anarchist exiles were playing an important part in the Maquis who were resisting Hitler on the French side of the Pyrenees.

Though never having any serious intention of fulfilling the dreams of the exiled Republicans by launching a military invasion of Spain, the British government was not slow to realize the potential of the anti-Fascist resistance. Hitler was the enemy, and Franco clearly Hitler's ally. The SIS officers cared little for the politics of those who resisted. If the Anarchists were the people who were the most serious and the most active, then it was to the Anarchists that they would go to for help in countering the schemes of the German intelligence services. The Anarchists were also useful in keeping open the escape routes for downed flyers, escaped POWs and Jews, across the Pyrenees.

In Spain, British Intelligence was well represented. The SIS Station Head in Madrid was Hamilton Stokes, assisted by Section Five representative Kenneth Benton (who subsequently headed the Information Research Department). Lieutenant-Commander Alan Hillgarth co-ordinated NID, SOE and SIS operations, while David Muirhead and David Babington-Smith headed the SOE contingent, and Michael Cresswell and Donald Darling were involved with MI9.

Sometime in 1941, SIS officers contacted members of the Anarchist resistance networks who, independently, were already involved in a two-way traffic of refugees across the border between Spain and France. But most of the Anarchist resistance scorned this contact because they did not have much faith in the Allies. Some, such as Amir Cruanes, ('the Sherif'), and Gines Urrea Pina (famous in Barcelona for having killed the public executioner before the Civil War) saw no problem. They would take the money and arms offered by the British agents, in return for escorting Allied airmen over the Pyrenees into Spain, or smuggling information and arms, but they would not be bought or controlled. The group around Pina carried out many daring raids, and was 'greatly favoured by British intelligence as a means of obtaining information by burglary about the Axis powers'.[5] Most of those actually involved are dead, or do not wish to record their impressions. Only one first-hand account has been published, called *Franco's Prisoner*, by Miguel Garcia, who had been involved in the co-operation between SIS and the Anarchist resistance. The author, in his book, records that at one point a British agent, an expert forger, was brought into Barcelona under the cover of the British Consulate. He then taught Miguel the art of producing licences, orders, visas, passports and pardons. Indeed, identification papers of all sorts were made which opened up a highway for Jewish refugees, British airmen, and volunteers for de Gaulle. Amongst those brought safely out was George Blake – whom we shall meet later.

The Anarchist historian of this period, Albert Meltzer, records that:

> Even those in the Resistance who never trusted the British agents, and who insisted on getting paid for any service they gave them, never believed that they could be double-crossed. Yet after a network of unions had been re-established in Spain during the war – and a Resistance built up without parallel in modern history, inside Spain – all the committees were destroyed. None of the militants ever saw cause and effect. Soon after the war, for instance, a meeting was called for by the British Embassy for the militants of the CNT to discuss the ANFD (Alliance of Democratic Forces) and the possibility of co-operation with the (pro-British) monarchists. CNT delegate Cipriano Mera reported that he could not see the point of it. A few weeks later the entire CNT committee was arrested. Cause and effect have not been seen to this day. How could it have been the British Embassy that was the traitor? Britain was 'democratic', Franco was 'Fascist'.[6]

After Mera had made his disagreement known, a message had been sent to SIS HQ, London, for advice. By now Philby was in charge of another important Section at the HQ. But in those days SIS HQ was very small indeed; all of the Section Heads knew each other, and subsequently discussed current events and problems – especially with officers who had had previous experience. As a former Head of Section Five, Philby was the man with the experience and was in a key position to influence events. For Philby and Moscow the Spanish Anarchists were ideological enemies, and therefore such an opportunity to neutralize them could not be wasted. The arrests of this group by the Spanish authorities dovetailed nicely with the interests of the Soviet Union, Spain and also the British government.

Some years earlier Gines Urrea Pina had remarked prophetically: 'If it suits them, they will sell us, no doubt about it.'[7] His lack of illusions with the democratic powers could not have been more correct.

In order to further integrate himself and add to his reputation in Section Five, Philby's Soviet superiors provided him and SIS with a major breakthrough in 1941. At that time Switzerland's neutrality was being used by Soviet agents. Two men, Alexander Rado (a Soviet agent) and Rudolf Rossler ran extremely efficient and widespread networks in Berne, Geneva and Lucerne. A Soviet link in London arranged for Philby to contact Alexander Rado. At the end of 1941 Philby subsequently suggested to his SIS superiors 'that Rado would supply information to the British military attaché in Berne',[8] Lieutenant-Colonel H. A. Cartwright, who was also SIS. In addition, Philby suggested that a Soviet agent named Christian Schneider (he did not reveal that she was a Soviet agent) was in touch with the Soviet network in Switzerland, and that the chief of this network was prepared to work for SIS, but for a price. In due course, SIS officer John Salter flew to Switzerland to make a thorough check. Eventually a positive decision was made. For the next two years SIS received valuable information from the Swiss-Soviet networks. But by 1943 the Swiss networks of Rado were closed down. However, Philby's 'contribution' in the form of his initial Soviet-sponsored suggestion 'had earned him the gratitude of SIS chiefs'.[9] Had the chiefs in fact known of

17

Philby's Soviet role, and that he was a mere conduit in the affair, their gratitude would not have been earned. However, during this period, the Soviets had far more to be grateful for from Philby, as he had access to the central archives of SIS at St Albans. This invaluable information contained codenames, the identification of networks and officers/agents in all parts of the world, including Soviet Russia.

According to Philby:

It was at this time that I nearly got into serious trouble ... There were a series of files in Registry known as source-books. These held the particulars and records of SIS agents operating abroad. It was natural for me to want information on the agents operating in the Iberian Peninsula, and my perusal of the source-books for Spain and Portugal whetted my appetite for more. I worked steadily through them, thus enlarging my knowledge of SIS activity as a whole. When I came to the source-book for the Soviet Union, I found that it consisted of two volumes. Having worked through them to my satisfaction, I returned them to Registry in the normal way.

About a week later, Bill telephoned to ask me for the second volume of the Russian source-book. After consulting my secretary, I called back to say that, according to our books it had been returned to Registry on such-and-such a date. After further fruitless search in Registry, Bill contested the accuracy of my records, and urged me to make a further investigation. I turned our office upside-down, with negative results. Bill and I met once or twice in the evening to discuss the mystery over a few pink gins.

He told me that the normal procedure on loss of a source-book was for him to report immediately to the Chief. I managed to stall him for a few days, during which time my alarm grew. I doubted whether the Chief would appreciate the excessive zeal which had led to my exhaustive study of source-books, especially as it had apparently resulted in the loss of one dealing with a country far outside the normal scope of my duties.

The lowering sky suddenly cleared. Bill telephoned me to offer a 'full, personal apology'. It seemed that one of his secretaries handling the source-books, wishing to save shelf space, had amalgamated the two volumes into one. She had then come over queer, and had gone home with a severe bout of flu. She had only just got back to

the office and, on being tackled by [Bill] Woodfield, had immediately remembered what she had done. I accepted the apology
gracefully, and suggested meeting again that evening. We did so,
and drowned the painful memory in a flood of pink gin.[10]

Following Philby's discovery of the names of British agents in
the Soviet Union, 'terrible consequences'[11] befell those agents.
At the end of the war, Philby's knowledge, gained from SIS
files, led to the deaths of agents in Hungary, Czechoslovakia,
Yugoslavia, Poland and Romania. In his cause for Communism,
Philby never wasted time and the countless deaths he caused
were of little, if any, consequence to him: the means justified
the end.

By 1943 Philby's field of responsibility was extended to
include North Africa, and later on Italy. In the meantime he had
become embroiled in office politics over Section Five's location
in terms of a choice between London or staying put at St
Albans; and the head of Section Five, Felix Cowgill wished to
remain at St Albans. On the other hand, Philby was 'wholly in
favour of [a] return to London', since such a move 'could only
assist in promoting an overall grasp of intelligence work'.[12]
What he meant was that such a move would have placed him
nearer to the Security Service and SIS HQs thus facilitating
access to more information. In the event, a free vote was taken
by the staff at St Albans, which resulted in a move to Ryder
Street, London being only two minutes away from the Security
Service HQ and fifteen minutes away from the SIS HQ at
Broadway.

Soon Philby found himself looking for fast promotion so that
he could head a new (anti-) Soviet Section. Long before the end
of the war, the senior officers in SIS, with a very good degree of
foresight, began to turn their thoughts to the next enemy:
Russia and Bolshevism.

So as soon as the defeat of Germany was in sight, SIS
introduced a small new section, known as Section IX, to study
previous pre-war records of Soviet and Communist activities. A
stopgap officer called Currie was put in charge, pending a

reduction in work, when a regular SIS officer would replace him. Philby desperately wanted the vacancy:

> For the next few weeks, virtually all of my discussions with my Soviet contact concerned the future of Section IX. I wrote several memoranda on the subject, which we analysed in exhaustive detail. The situation, as I explained it to them, held out two possible solutions: on retirement, Currie could be replaced by another officer, or his section could be merged with Section V.
> Cowgill had no doubt that the second solution would be adopted. He would talk airily of the days when we got rid of old Currie and really got down to the Communist Job.[13]

Philby's Soviet contact wanted to know if Philby would be offered a senior position in the section. Philby thought that he would but he could not be certain. The contact informed Philby that he: 'must do everything but everything to ensure that [he] become Head of Section IX, whether or not it merged with Section V.' This meant that Cowgill had to go, and Philby was ready to play any dirty or loathsome trick to get rid of him. This he initiated by seeing his old patron, Colonel Vivian, and suggested that Cowgill was not loyal to Vivian. Unfortunately, for Cowgill, who in Philby's own words 'sometimes seemed bent on self-destruction, chose this critical moment to try to propel the Chief into a wholly unnecessary row with Edgar Hoover', the head of the FBI in America. Cowgill had drafted a two-page letter for the Chief to sign which was 'a tirade against Hoover's regular practice of sacrificing intelligence needs for political advantage in Washington'.[14] Vivian, as a result was out for Cowgill's blood, and with the letter as ammunition, Philby lobbied for support against Cowgill, and gained it from many quarters.

Subsequently Philby was summoned by Vivian, and told that his name had been put forward as a successor to Currie. Following this meeting Philby was interviewed, and accepted as Head of Section IX. At last Philby had made it! He was even able to draft his own charter for the Section, which would be signed by the Chief. This charter gave Philby:

1. Responsibility for the collection and interpretation of information concerning Soviet and Communist espionage and subversion in all parts of the world outside British territory.
2. Maintain the closest liaison for the reciprocal exchange of intelligence on these subjects with MI5.[15]

Now Philby was the highest placed Soviet agent in SIS.

Being in charge of Section IX meant that he had to move from Ryder Street to the SIS HQ, at 55 Broadway, where he devoted himself wholeheartedly to his work, and was very pleased with what he had achieved:

> I had enjoyed easy access to the heart of SIS. Now I was sitting right in the middle of it.

His office was on the seventh floor just down the corridor from that of his old patron, Colonel Vivian. The building was officially described as a Government Communications Bureau. Within a few months of arrival Philby had recruited new staff; and by the end of twelve months he had a range of staff working for him, of whom some were on the left.

Philby, of course, was exposing every vital detail of the rapidly growing SIS departments to the Soviets, and had 'permanent access to many state secrets, and [was] able to procure unlimited information for Moscow'.[16] In order to achieve such total access he worked long hours: a colleague is quoted as saying, 'Sometimes I'd be back at the office until nine or ten o'clock, and on the way out I'd pass Kim's room. He'd be sweating over papers.'[17] The reason for these late hours is apparent. Philby on many occasions used to repeatedly countermand a strict SIS internal rule to his staff over the fact that each desk should be locked by each member responsible for it upon finishing work. Evidently, Philby used to say: 'Don't worry about that. I'll be working late tonight and I'll see to the locking up.' One secretary recollected:

> It used to worry me at the time. I didn't like leaving my desk open [unlocked]. But he was so charming and I couldn't resist anything he asked.[18]

Since Philby had knowledge of hundreds of SIS staff, their cover was blown for life, and would have been recognized by the RIS upon arriving at any foreign posting. Philby also pried for his RIS masters when he travelled to SIS stations abroad. He visited France and Germany (after the end of the war), Italy and Greece, which gave him an insight into various types of SIS organizations in the field. Back in the UK, Philby and his allies at the SIS HQ recommended changes: the creation of five Directorates.

1. Finance and administration.
2. Production.
3. Requirements.
4. Training and development.
5. War planning.

A bulky report was prepared for presentation to the Chief although he did not accept all of the recommendations, but, by and large, the outline was adopted as a basic pattern. Philby had no cause for dissatisfaction; after all, it was decided to abolish Section Five. During this period, RIS had little cause for dissatisfaction with Philby and his Section. After all, according to Philby: 'During my period of service [in Sections Five and IX], there was no single case of a consciously conceived operation against Soviet intelligence bearing fruit.' He made sure of that.

THE VOLKOV EPISODE

During August 1945 Philby's cover was almost blown by a Russian defector called Konstantin Volkov, a Vice-Consul (RIS) attached to the Soviet Consulate-General in Istanbul, who had approached a Mr Page, his British counterpart, and asked for political asylum in Britain for he and his wife in return for important information. Soon details about Volkov, plus a document, typed by Volkov, arrived in London. A crucial clause in the document offered:

Files and documents concerning very important Soviet agents in important establishments in London. Judging by the Cryptonyms [the code-names in RIS cables between London and Moscow], there are at present seven such agents, five are in British intelligence, and two in the Foreign Office. I know, for instance, that one of these agents is fulfilling the duties of Head of Department of British counter-intelligence.[19]

When details crossed Philby's desk: 'He immediately identified the agent fulfilling the duties of Head of a Department of British counter-intelligence as himself [and] alerted his Russian controller in London.'[20] Interestingly enough, Volkov had demanded that details between Turkey and London not be sent by telegraph on the ground that the Russians had broken a variety of British cyphers. Instead, details were sent by diplomatic bag to SIS HQ, London – to be read by, of all people, Philby!

It was immediately decided that information should go no further than Philby. Action had to be taken to protect him, and to ensure Volkov's silence. Philby recounted that:

That evening, I worked late. The situation seemed to call for urgent action of an extra-curricular nature. Next morning, I reported to the Chief that, although we had several Volkovs on file, none of them matched our man in Istanbul. I repeated my view that the case was of great potential importance. Dwelling on the delays involved in communication by bag, I recommended rather diffidently, that someone fully briefed should be sent out to take charge of the case on the spot.

Eventually, Philby manoeuvred himself into the position whereby he would go to Turkey and take charge, and later, after many delays, arrived in Turkey. In the meantime, Volkov was seized, strapped to a stretcher, and was removed from Istanbul by air to Moscow. There he was terminated. Philby afterwards managed to extricate himself from any blame over the Volkov affair. The diplomat who had initially interviewed Volkov wanted to know why there had been a very long time-gap which had probably delayed the whole operation. Why, Page asked, was someone not sent earlier? 'Sorry,' Philby explained. 'It would have interfered with leave arrangements.'

Had Volkov exposed Philby, it would have been a great blow to the Russians and a defeat in the East-West espionage battle. As it was, Philby's presence in the heart of SIS 'enabled the Russians to plan their cold war espionage as a logically integrated operation'[21] Philby caused the death of Volkov, but this was only one in a long line of deaths to be caused by him. But even after Philby's unmasking, and the revealing of the enormity of his betrayals, including countless deaths, former officers who had known, and had even worked with him, did not fully denounce him.

Malcolm Muggeridge, for example, stated that:

It would be equally untrue for me now to say Philby's double-cross [towards Felix Cowgill] fills me with abhorrence. If I were to run into him, I would, I am sure, pass as agreeable an evening with him as I ever did when we were both in Section Five.[22]

And Graham Greene also stated that:

I liked him [Philby]. I've often asked myself what I would have done if I'd discovered he was a [Soviet] secret agent at the time ... I think, perhaps, if in a drunken moment he had slipped a hint, I would have given him twenty-four hours to get clear then reported him.[23]

The two views are hard to reconcile. Muggeridge and Greene[24] have been for a long time cognizant of Philby's treachery, deceit, adultery, and behaviour which led to countless deaths and imprisonments of captured agents.

Following the Volkov affair, Philby was not surprised when General Sinclair summoned him towards the end of 1946 and informed that he was in line for a tour of duty overseas. The first posting was to take charge of the SIS Station in Turkey, having its HQ in Istanbul. At that time, Istanbul was the main southern base for intelligence work and operations directed against the Soviet Union and the Soviet satellite countries of the Balkans and Central Europe. Philby was fairly pleased:

> Although I would no longer be right in the middle of my main field of interest, I would not be so far off-centre.[25]

He also had other reasons for being pleased: in addition to knowing that at least six more Soviet agents were placed in SIS/MI5, he was also pleased with the progress of George Blake.

3

ENTER GEORGE BLAKE

Some degree of controversy and conflict exists over the relationship of Philby and Blake. For some reason, the authors who have written about Philby have not concentrated, or, it seems, discovered anything on the duo. Indeed, if one reads what has been written on the two RIS agents, one would not suspect any interrelationship in terms of spying and collaborative activities between the two.

> Philby knew of but had barely met [Blake] whose espionage exploits [in Germany] for Soviet Russia were unknown to him.
> Andrew Boyle, *The Climate of Treason*

> Philby had no knowledge that Blake was a KGB agent. Nor it seems, did Blake have any certain knowledge concerning Philby's KGB role.
> Chapman Pincher, *Their Trade is Treachery*

> The two operated separately and knew nothing of each other's double role.
> Patrick Seale and Maureen McConville,
> *Philby, the Long Road to Moscow*

However, the combination of Philby and Blake working together in the mid-1950s was a very deadly one indeed, and led to the deaths of Allied agents in the Ukraine.

The backgrounds of Philby and Blake differ. Whereas Philby was born into an upper-middle-class British family, Blake was born into a middle-class Dutch family on 11 November, 1922, and named George (in honour of King George V) Bihar. Blake's family on his father's side was of Jewish origin; although his mother's side were staunch and conservative Protestants. George was brought up under strict Lutheran instruction. He was sent to a select school at The Hague, where according to a maid in the Bihar family, he was a 'rather lonely little boy'.[1] At the age of sixteen he became a pupil at the Rotterdam High School Meer Urtgebreid Lager Onderwijs. From childhood he developed an almost accentless English, and had also acquired a very good mastery of German and French.

Whilst he was still a pupil at high school in 1940, Holland was overrun by German troops and subjugated by Germany. Prior to the Dutch surrender, Rotterdam was mercilessly bombed by the German air force until the city was one huge conflagration. During one attack, some 60,000 people were killed or wounded. Needless to say, Blake and the other survivors did not forget or forgive the Germans. Unfortunately for Blake, one of his grandmother's neighbours who belonged to the Dutch Nazi Party denounced him to the German Gestapo as a Britisher. He was therefore arrested and was taken north of Amsterdam to an internment camp at Sckoorl near Alkmaar. Even though the camp was heavily guarded by SS troops, he made a daring escape and he headed eastwards to his uncle's home at Warnveld. There he hid for a while until his uncle was able to arrange for a safer hiding place with a farmer.

At the age of eighteen, Blake became one of the leaders of the first local resistance group, when he assumed the name of Max van Vries. He was a farm-hand by day, but at night he 'and his men met to plan resistance and sabotage actions against the Nazi invaders'.[2] Since his group did not possess arms or explosives, they limited their actions to cutting telephone lines, slashing the tyres of German military vehicles, and strewing nails in the path of enemy army convoys. Eventually, the

Gestapo's security police, became aware of his minor saboteur activities and put a price on his head. But he avoided capture and fled to the town of Limburg to join a major countrywide resistance organization called Orde Dienst which mainly had as its members disbanded officers from the Dutch military services. This resistance organization worked closely with the Dutch government in exile based in London, and with SIS and SOE. Initially, the organization did not attempt any spectacular actions. Eventually Blake became a very junior participant in the link between the Dutch resistance and SOE, and had volunteered for several dangerous missions, the result of which was that the Germans began looking for a young terrorist called Max van Vries. When Blake got in contact with SIS Commander R. W. Child who was in Holland, Child soon warned him that the Gestapo was looking for him, and urgently advised him to leave Holland using SOE escape routes and 'safe houses'.

Blake escaped via Belgium, France and Spain – along one of the Anarchist-organized routes as mentioned in the previous chapter. While in Spain, Blake wrote to the British Embassy, who sent an official to take him to Madrid, and then on to Gibraltar, where he was interrogated by Major Donald Darling of MI9 (which was linked to Section Five at SIS HQ, then headed by Philby). Once Blake was cleared, he commenced his journey to England and was held in custody for several days while the Security Service and Special Branch officers examined him. He was able to refer to Commander Child, and was soon cleared.

Now in London, Blake once more met Commander Child, and upon Child's advice volunteered for the Royal Navy. He became an ordinary seaman, a few days prior to his twenty-first birthday. However, he did not remain a seaman for too long, for once his fluency of three languages was discovered he was recommended for a commission and was sent on an officer's training course in HMS *King Alfred* at Hove. By the spring of 1944 he had completed the course, with excellent marks, and was a sub-lieutenant. In May 1944, he was posted as an interpreter to the staff of Supreme Allied Expeditionary Force (SHAEF) and subsequently to the Allied Naval Expeditionary Force (ANCXF) at Southwick House, north of Portsmouth. His duties included the translation and interpretation of German documents captured by SOE and SIS agents. His reports and translations were of a good standard, so much so that he was commended for his work by Montgomery's Chief of Staff, Major-General de Guingand.

His excellent work did not go unnoticed by SIS or Philby. When Blake's work (and his personal file) crossed Philby's desk, he was 'talent spotted as a possible SIS recruit for counter-espionage in Germany'.[3] Accordingly, Blake: '...was summoned by a senior intelligence officer and asked whether he wanted to become a counter-espionage officer against the Soviets, and he agreed immediately.'[4]

It was because of this promotion, that at the end of the war Blake found himself in charge of his own naval intelligence unit, where he laid his hands on as many U-boat commanders and technical experts as possible – in order to interrogate them and compile a record of Germany's conduct of the war at sea. This information was important and indeed was required by the Allied governments for use at the Nuremburg trials, 1945–46. Blake proved to be very successful in securing the required information. Towards the end of his time in Germany, he showed an interest in learning the Russian language and when interviewed at the Foreign Office in the spring of 1947 '...discussed with a senior official his plan to learn Russian...'[5] His idea was accepted, and he was told that upon completion of the course he would be given a Foreign Service appointment in the Consular Branch – in reality, he was to become an SIS officer.

Following demobilization from the Navy, Blake arrived at Cambridge University in October 1947, having been accepted by Downing College for a course in Russian. 'His tutors at Downing were impressed by the ease and eagerness with which their pupil absorbed the essentials of this difficult language ...

[he had a] ... remarkable acumen for linguistics...'[6] Indeed, one female, who taught Russian, was very impressed.

During his stay at Cambridge, Blake visited London at least twice a month and he popped in and out of Section IX at SIS HQ. Even though he and Philby had barely met, Philby, disappointed that Burgess no longer had the run of Hector McNeil's secret files (he had been the Foreign Office minister's personal secretary) was able to '...console himself that George Blake ... was taking a crash course in Russian at Downing College, Cambridge.'[7] Philby had reason to be pleased, for Blake was to become a most dangerous RIS agent when he was employed as a conduit passing valuable secrets to Philby from the Foreign Office, in and around 1954. At this time Philby, prior to his posting to Turkey, was attached to a training section for an officer's course. Having completed the course, he visited his father en route to Istanbul.

PHILBY 1947

Having arrived in Turkey, Philby found himself in a country in the cold war theatre between East and West. Turkey also occupied a long border with the Soviet Union as well as bordering with Communist Bulgaria. By 1947, the country had become a haven for spies and agents who had arrived from Poland, Yugoslavia, Bulgaria and Albania. According to Philby:

A surprising number of Bulgarians, Yugoslavs and Romanians claimed to have established espionage organisations in their own [Communist] countries before passing into exile themselves. They were more than willing to put such networks at our disposal, provided we [SIS and CIA] put up the necessary funds for activating them.[8]

Providing such information on the networks, and the identities of agents to Philby, sealed the agents' death warrants.

Turkey was now somewhat over-represented by the influx of members of the RIS, SIS and CIA. Istanbul thronged with Soviet spies, and Ankara was accredited with nine British military attachés and their assistants, including six full colonels; all found themselves involved in a spate of travelling between Ankara and Istanbul. Back in Istanbul, Philby found himself with several 'acting' First and Second Secretaries, plus consuls: '...the great majority of SIS officers abroad [had] been posted as First, Second, or Third Secretaries, according to seniority.'[9]

SIS HQ, London, had told Philby that his first priority was the Soviet Union and therefore he concentrated much of his time on a personal reconnaissance of Soviet frontier areas which offered the greatest possibility of infiltrating agents into the Soviet Union. During his jeep journeys across the wilder parts of Anatolia, Philby sent long reports by radio and diplomatic bags to his SIS chiefs. 'As before, he had arranged with his Soviet controllers what information was appropriate to convey, and they agreed that he could report on some of the less harmful activities of Soviet agents, to keep London satisfied.'[10] On the other hand, Philby fed his Soviet controllers with most useful information: 'The RAF lost at least one aircraft on the Turkish-Russian border in consequence.'[11] Following one journey, Philby called at the office of Tefik Bey who was employed by the Turkish Security Inspectorate. At the end of their talks, Philby came to the conclusion that what was required was the establishment and placing of resident agents in Erivan, Tiflis, and the eastern parts of the Black Sea. Philby, therefore, suggested to SIS HQ that Georgian and Armenian émigré communities be appraised by SIS stations in Paris, Beirut, Washington and other centres, in order to locate and find agents of sufficient ability to be trained to SIS requirements. Subsequently they could take part in OPERATION SPYGLASS.

The proposal for OPERATION SPYGLASS was favourably received by SIS HQ. Accordingly, an SIS officer was sent from London to Paris to meet a man called Jordania, a sometime Head of the Independent Republic of Georgia, who promised to find men and indeed two men were trained in London. In the meantime, Philby put the finishing touches to OPERATION SPYGLASS, described as being 'extraordinarily interesting' by SIS HQ.

By 1948, all plans were made and ready: two trained men arrived in Istanbul from Paris. (Both had been born in Paris, and had known Georgia only by hearsay.) Upon their arrival they travelled to Erzurum, to be met by Tefik Bey, who had made all the arrangements for infiltrating them over the frontier. This information had been released to Philby. Under the escort of a Turkish officer, the two men were taken to the border, and within minutes of crossing one man was cut down by a burst of fire, and the other man: '...was last seen striding through a sparse wood away from the Turkish frontier. He was never heard of again.'[12] Once again, Philby was able to credit himself with the deaths of two anti-Soviet enemies. However, this was not to be the last incidence of such a betrayal of Allied agents. Philby was to become embroiled in the long-running Albanian operations between 1949 and 1952.

4

THE MERCHANT OF DEATH

Philby arrived in Washington in September, 1949, with the rank of First Secretary, SIS liaison officer, with the newly formed (1947) Central Intelligence Agency and the FBI. A special relationship had emerged between the CIA and SIS. Somehow the CIA looked upon SIS 'with some awe'.[1] Philby's arrival in Washington had been preceded by a considerable reputation. Some of the Americans whom he was to work with, had known him during the war and assessed him as: 'a rising star of British counter-espionage; [a] victor in the SIS "palace revolution"; a specialist in anti-Soviet operations.'[2]

He had a very important position which included access to the Head of the CIA, General Bedell Smith and to the Head of the FBI, J. Edgar Hoover; and as a result was a party to planning and policy, plus details of what the CIA knew about RIS operations. Since Philby had been cleared to speak with Bedell Smith he was also: 'cleared right through every department and merely by drinking around he could have learned more about the agency and its operations than any man except the Director and perhaps one or two of his assistants.'[3] As to what he could, and was, able to learn, one former CIA officer explained: 'The sky was the limit. He would have known as much as he wanted to find out.'[4] In fact, he gained information on every CIA/SIS operation in Germany, Poland, China and the Ukraine and

33

passed it onto his Soviet controller. He was responsible for the disappearance of a score of American and British officers/agents sent into the Balkans through Albania, Italy, Turkey and Greece between 1949 and 1951, or until the operations were cancelled because of an obvious leak.

Philby attended several joint British-American meetings to co-ordinate respective operations into the Soviet Union 'and to prevent any confusion or overlap in our air-dispatch of agents into the Baltic states and the Ukraine'.[5] One meeting was recalled by the former CIA officer Harry Rositzke, concerning operations into Lithuania:

> Philby sat at one corner of the conference table flanked by the British Soviet experts from London. At one point I raised the question: Can we determine whether or not the British agents then reporting by radio from Lithuania were under KGB control? Philby did not offer an opinion in the ensuing discussion.[6]

For Philby, it mattered little what happened to the captured agents – provided he was not implicated in any way. Even before he became Head of Section IX, Philby was feeding details to the Russians about British agents in Russia. Blunt did not do too badly either. 'Some of Blunt's wartime knowledge may very well have brought about the deaths or very unpleasant lives of some of our friends in Eastern Europe,'[7] opined the former SIS Vice-Chief, George Kennedy Young. During this period, Blunt controlled Leo Long who 'would certainly have known the identity of agents and informers in his work in the intelligence division of the British Control Commission for Germany [including Austria] after the war'.[8] It appears that Burgess (who recruited Blunt for the RIS) also effected the deaths of agents. Former SIS officer Montague Woodhouse holds 'him equally guilty, if indirectly, with Philby etc., since he recruited many of them [agents who became victims] in the first place'.[9]

Upon reading the accounts of betrayals and deaths, one can only concur with Harry Rositzke that the damage Philby did to

CIA/SIS is 'incalculable'[10] and that the deaths caused by Philby, Blunt, Burgess and possibly Maclean are 'most horrifying'.[11] Fortunately, for the CIA/SIS officers and agents, Philby did not take advantage of every opportunity he had. In 1949 he was approached by Commander Courtney of Naval Intelligence at SIS HQ. Courtney suggested to Philby the sending of 'couriers into Russia by submarine'.[12] Philby totally disagreed with the idea and would have nothing to do with it, for obvious reasons. Had he agreed and the suggestion been actualized, Philby would have arranged for the couriers' capture, but could not have afforded any subsequent investigation as it would have pointed to him.

THE 'RAT LINE'

In Washington Philby was very busy and spent most of his time with the Office of Strategic Operations (OSO) headed by James Jesus Angleton and the Office of Policy Co-ordination (OPC) headed by Frank Wisner. Wisner was a former World War II Navy man who hailed from a wealthy southern family. He soon discovered that the naval service was not exciting enough, and joined the OSS, at that time a new independent US intelligence agency. The remainder of the war found him as an agent in the Balkans, engaged in clandestine activities both in Turkey and Romania. Post-war legal work was too mundane, and Wisner longed to be back in 'the field'. Not long after, he became an assistant to Allen Dulles, of the OSS. Following the dissolution of the OSS, Wisner joined the Pentagon's War Department Detachment, subsequently known as the Department of the Army Detachment of DAD. 'DAD was the umbrella organization for all non-military cover.'[13] During this time, the Allies were highly concerned about the Soviet Union. According to Jim Miland, a former American Counter-Intelligence Corps operative, formally based in Germany:

We knew very little about Russia, we knew damn little about their

35

army, we knew very little about their tactics, we knew very little about their manuals, mode of operations – that sort of thing. So there was considerable pressure on the intelligence community to gather information ... the methodologies that [UK-US used] were [not] any different, because we were in touch with the British, the French and all sorts of intelligence. I think there was an attitude that you'd do almost anything within reason ... to collect intelligence.[14]

In 1948 many Western intelligence agencies believed that a Soviet attack on Western Europe was imminent, and the agencies had been put on a war footing. Wisner's frame of reference was to plan and organize an underground network of commando units to hamper and slow down any Soviet advance. 'His weapons included propaganda, economic warfare, sabotage and subversion against hostile states, including assistance to underground resistance groups in Eastern Europe.'[15] The above frame of reference had been given to Wisner under the OPC charter which had been issued by the US State Department. He was particularly interested in the latter part of the charter which was concerned with the recruitment of an anti-Communist guerrilla army to fight against the Soviet bloc. Wisner already had a list of Romanians who were opposed to the Soviet Union. This list contained Nazi collaborators, and soon was to contain men, many of whom were accused war criminals, from all across Eastern Europe. At the end of the war, numerous Nazi war criminals were to be found in Western POW camps. The Western intelligence services of America, France and Britain (particularly Britain, being given a first choice) took a considerable interest in potential recruits. In the words of Jim Miland: 'You'd do almost anything within reason ... to collect intelligence.' But before examining some of the people who were recruited (Philby was a recruiter), we shall look at the history of the Nazi collaborators.

When Germany invaded the Soviet Union, victorious German troops were met by willing collaborators, especially in Byelorussia and the Ukraine. The Byelorussian ranks included the cream of their intelligentsia, who assisted the new German administration both military and political. Some joined the dreaded SS. A special test was employed by the SS for its Byelorussian collaborators:

> Only those who assisted the Einsatzgruppen [task force] would be permitted to become part of the civilian administration [in the conquered areas] to be established in the wake of the advancing Wehrmacht and Waffen-SS troops.[16]

The Einsatzgruppen were, in fact, special mobile units dealing with the liquidation of Communist officials, partisans, saboteurs, as well as Jews on the Eastern front. Upon conquering new areas, the Byelorussian collaborators singled out particular people for execution. Stanislaw Stankievich was a collaborator who controlled the town of Borissow. He had been picked by Dr Franz Six, SS leader and head of Vorkommando for Einsatzgruppe B, to assist Einsatzgruppe B, and had ordered all Jews in Borissow to be resettled in the poorest areas. Stankievich gave orders to Sergeant Soennecken to murder about 7,000 Jewish men, women and children. Only a handful of temporarily essential Jews were to be ignored. By sunrise on the following morning of 20 October, 1941 all the Jews had been rounded up.

> The first contingent, about 20 men, were made to jump into the pits after taking off all but their underwear. They were shot from above. Of course these dead and half-dead people were lying pell-mell. The next victims had to line them up so as to gain as much space as possible. Then it continued as above. When the bottom row of the mass grave was full, the [remaining] Jews had to put a layer of sand over the bodies. The most horrible scenes are said to have taken place in these mass graves ... the Russian policemen were given a great deal of liquor...[17]

The killing went on throughout the day. Stankievich had underestimated the manpower needed for the operation, and German troops had to be called out to guard the ghetto so more policemen could be sent to deal with the crowds at the execution grounds. Too

37

many trucks arrived at the same time, and there were not enough men to direct the unloading. A few Jews tried to escape, but most were killed before they reached the woods. Others were too frightened to move until prodded towards the graves. Many accepted the futility of resistance and quietly followed the line to the pit to which they were assigned. Some of the guards raped the younger women before forcing them into the pits. Heads were smashed by rifle butts, and bodies were mutilated. Autopsies conducted after the war showed that babies, out of sheer savagery or to save ammunition, had been thrown into the pits and buried alive.[18]

Borissow was only the beginning: similar events occurred in the ghettos of Minsk and Baranovichi. Such was the degree of inhumanity that by the beginning of 1943 most of the areas originally inhabited by Byelorussian Jewry had been exterminated save for a few thousand specialists and technicians in special ghettos and concentration camps because of their specialist expertise of skills. One such concentration camp was Koldichevo, in south-west Byelorussia. Very few inmates escaped from this institution, but Soloman Schiadow was one and subsequently he described the inside conditions:

The Byelorussian guards were so brutal that the prisoners prayed that they would be replaced by Germans. One day a Byelorussian caught a youngster looking at the sky as planes flew overhead and accused the prisoner of attempting to signal enemy aircraft. The guard ordered several other Jews to hold the youth down over a table. He took out his knife and began to carve large steaks out of the living flesh of the younger man, as if he were a butcher calmly working on a side of beef.[19]

Before, during and after 1944, when Soviet troops regained territories, the Byelorussian and Ukrainian collaborators quickly moved to the British, French and American fronts. These collaborators had not only 'served' in the USSR, but also the Nazis in the Waffen-Genadier division der SS, Russicha No. 2. This regiment included Byelorussian and Ukrainian units who were later transferred to Italy as part of the 29th Waffen SS Division.

Members also went to France as part of the 30th Division. Many defected to American troops. Other defectors moved from the Soviet Union: Byelorussian and Ukrainian fugitives escaped to the British zone of Höxter and were separated into a regional category and placed in separate POW camps. Eight hundred collaborators moved from Minsk to Germany and nearly all eventually went to America.

Following their screening by the British authorities, some members of the more numerous Ukrainian groups combined into one, a sort of umbrella organization, KTs AB, and with official British permission from SIS formed HQs in Paris, London, Munich and Rome. These members were protected because, after the war ended, Soviet emissaries searched POW camps for Byelorussian and Ukrainian fugitives for repatriation. If captured, once back in Russia they would have been put to death or exiled in Siberia.

Much publicity has been generated over how Klaus Barbie[20] was ferreted via a 'rat line' from Germany to Latin America. Yet another 'rat line' to America existed and has been described in *The Belarus Secret* by Professor John Loftus. However, no publicity has been given by the British media about the ultra-secret 'rat line' between Germany and Britain.

SIS, in the form of Philby's Section IX, was given the first choice of any captive (German or non-German) Nazi war criminal and/or collaborator, of whom an important handful were moved to Britain. Philby was a chief recruiter. On the following pages, we shall examine three of the men who passed through British hands on the 'rat line'; all of whom were recruited by Section IX, headed by Philby.

Mikolai Abramtchik

Dr Abramtchik was recruited by German intelligence whilst in Byelorussia despite the fact that he had been active in the Communist youth organization there. As a collaborator he worked secretly for the Gestapo and the SS. Before the Red Army captured Berlin, the Byelorussian puppet government had fled to the West, and Abramtchik made his way to the French. He and the Western-influenced Byelorussians volunteered their services and assets to the French Secret Service, who were willing to overlook wartime collaboration, and approved the establishment of a Polish military mission in Paris – a cover for Franco – for the recruitment of leading fugitive members of the Belarus SS Brigade. Then Abramtchik was recruited by Philby, along with other associates who were later discovered to be former Communists. Indeed, his organization had the most ex-Nazi collaborators. Section IX arranged for them to parachute into Byelorussia. Because of Philby's involvement, upon their return all were captured or shot. The Abramtchik faction began to collapse. But here Philby played a major coup. He offloaded the Communist-infested Abramtchik organization on the eager Frank Wisner, emphasizing the extensive espionage network that Abramtchik was supposedly developing in Poland. The sardonic Philby must have smiled to himself as he handed over the hollow shells of his Eastern European operations to Wisner. Philby, who certainly was no fool, in his memoirs dismissed Wisner as 'a youngish man for so responsible a job, balding and running self-importantly to fat'.[21]

Radislaw Ostrowsky
He, too, was left-wing and a member of the Byelorussian Peasants and Workers Party (The Granada); he also spoke fluent Russian. Following the German occupation, Ostrowsky and his men ran everything for the Germans: Byelorussian police patrolled the streets of Minsk. Hundreds of people were informed upon by Ostrowsky and his associates and were duly sent off to concentration camps; factories were reopened utilizing Jews and Soviet POWs under slave labour projects. Minsk became a highly important staging post for the German advance upon Moscow, where upon surrender Ostrowsky expected to become mayor. The ultimate aim of the Byelorussians was to attain a separate independent state.

Germany was willing to allow a limited form of national

autonomy and Ostrowsky was selected by the SS to head the new regime. He had only six months to prove that his quisling government was worthy of continued SS backing, and therefore spread propaganda amongst the peasants calling upon them to fight for 'order and peace' not only for themselves but for the Germans as a Soviet victory would mean 'the return of Communism'. Referring to past atrocities against the peasantry, he blamed 'Jew-Bolsheviks' instead of the Nazis.

Whenever Ostrowsky visited Berlin, he and his government were warmly received by the Fuhrer and his party. When defeat was in sight, Ostrowsky and his faction moved to the British zone of Höxter. Realizing that the Allies could not officially embrace a Nazi-created government, despite now a government in exile, Ostrowsky created a front organization: the Byelorussian Central Representation (BCR), which originally under him had been the Byelorussian Central Council (BCC) – during the war, this organization had raised sixty-five battalions for a national militia, later formed into the Belarus SS brigade. Under SIS protection the BCR formed a world-wide network of branches in England, Canada, Australia, Brazil and Germany. Once again, Philby had recruited a fugitive.

Across in Paris, Abramtchik bitterly attacked Ostrowsky's faction. Likewise Ostrowsky, known as 'a butcher' by SIS, attacked Abramtchik by repeatedly charging that many of Abramtchik's associates were former Communists and that his group had been riddled with Soviet informers. When faced with these charges, Frank Wisner went to Philby for his comment. Philby, naturally, gave him assurances that Ostrowsky's warnings 'were merely the sour grapes of a disaffected politician'. However, the charges in later years were corroborated by the CIC, whose records showed that several pro-Soviet agents were uncovered; other security agencies discovered that one of Abramtchik's deputies had been trained as a security officer by the Soviets and that several Byelorussians (in a network) passed sensitive information to the Eastern bloc intelligence services.

General Gehlen of German intelligence believed the Byelorussian émigrés who had recently collaborated with the Germans; he considered that they were more in touch with the thinking of the populations within the Soviet bloc. Gehlen, therefore, immediately recruited Ostrowsky and his faction once they had been dropped by Philby. Ostrowsky and his group were also taken over by Frank Wisner; later SIS moved Ostrowsky to Argentina in 1950, out of the way for the time being. However, in 1952, he was subsequently moved to London to work with the OPC and SIS in a new attempt to penetrate the Iron Curtain. In Ostrowsky's opinion, it was his Nazis, and not those of Abramtchik, who offered the best opportunity and chance of penetrating the Soviet Union. He did not have to wait too long – even though the results were to prove a disaster.

Stanislaw Stankievich

The arch-butcher Stankievich even surpassed Ostrowsky by his barbarous actions. We have seen when he ruled the city of Borissow his ordering the extermination of innocent Jews, and providing the necessary manpower for such atrocities. At the end of the war, Stankievich moved across into the British sector, to join Abramtchik's organization. He was hired as an English language teacher for POW camps. Because he was part of the faction headed by Abramtchik, he became part of the 'package' recruited by Philby. Subsequently, he was a leading figure in Abramtchik's organization, becoming its vice-president. He also became chairman of the Learned Council of the Institute of Russian Research in Munich, placed under Radio Liberty (99.9% of its funds were from the CIA). 'After Stankievich was overheard bragging about the mass executions at Borissow, one of the other émigrés asked an OPC liaison man whether it was wise to place a notorious war criminal in such a prominent position. The discussion was cut short. Stankievich was credited with being an important source.'[22] In the late 1950s he was allowed to enter America, and eventually became a naturalized citizen on 8 March 1969. His entry had been organized by Frank Wisner's staff, who had sent a letter to the Immigration and Naturalization Service requesting that Stankievich be issued a re-entry permit to facilitate his leaving the country for Germany. Over the following ten years, he travelled repeatedly to and from Germany. This level of freedom was excellent considering that he was a high-ranking Nazi collaborator and a self-confessed murderer.

In 1945 'leading Byelorussian Nazis were transported to London ... given a stipend of five hundred pounds, provided with police transportation and employed as government translators as cover for their covert operations.'[23] Philby's Section IX had arranged, under the cover of the anti-Bolshevic Bloc of Nations (ABN), to bring across such men as Stankievich to Edinburgh for a convention of right-wing anti-Communists. Another participant was Mikolai Abramtchik. His staff were given space for an HQ at the Francis Ckryuna Library in London – a private research group. Their files included a complete set of Nazi propaganda newspapers published during the war, complete with names and photographs of the collaborators.

ALBANIA

On 5 September, 1949, at the first meeting, in Washington, of the Council of the North Atlantic Organization (NATO), British Labour Minister Ernest Bevin proposed to institute a counter-revolution in Albania. A briefing paper prepared by the State Department for his visit declared:

> The US would like to see the present Moscow-dominated regime disappear, but the question would then be what kind of regime would take its place. Most preferable would be a Western-oriented regime such as is desired by the Albanian National Committee, a group of exiled leaders now in Rome and Paris. It could not be expected that Albania would be governed democratically.

43

Recommendations:
That the US act in co-ordination with the UK and France in the Albanian situation as it develops;
That the US do what it can ... to weaken the position of the present Soviet-dominated regime in Albania;
That the US give moral support to pro-Albanian elements.[24]

Bevin had powerful and influential backers, including US Secretary of State Dean Acheson, the American Chiefs of Staff, the Dulles brothers, who were fanatical adherents of covert programmes, together with such OPC men as William Colby, Frank Wisner, Richard Bissell and Frank Lindsay. The CIA held James Jesus Angleton and Richard Helms (later head of the CIA) who had supportive views. Across in Britain the influential Conservative politician Julian Amery, a former member of SOE, in an early speech in the House of Commons summarized his enduring convictions:

> It must be the task of statesmanship, while American supremacy persists, to obtain from Russia a settlement which will ensure its retreat behind the Curzon line, and the breaking of the monopoly power by the Communist parties in the countries of Eastern Europe.

His ideas struck a sympathetic chord with British ministers. A new Foreign Office unit was set up, chaired by Gladwyn Jebb, followed by a Cold War Sub-Committee, holding the brief of finding ways for liberating the Soviet satellites by any means short of war. One member, Ivone Kirkpatrick had a brainwave: a civil war in Albania. The Committee agreed and turned to Amery who had been approached by Major-General Sir Colin Gubbins formerly of SIS Section D.

Meanwhile, Colonel Neil McLean, who was Amery's old friend, had also been busy. Frank Wisner had flown to London and whilst lunching with McLean at Buck's Club on 15 April, they discussed a proposed guerrilla training base at Malta. Two weeks later, McLean once more discussed the plan, but over dinner this time with Shadow Foreign Secretary Anthony Eden. Concurrently, Bevin asked: 'Are there any kings around that could be put in [to Albania]?' Amery replied that there was such a king, Zog of Albania, with whom Amery had fought in Albania, and he had again contacted him at Alexandria in 1949. In the event, Britain and America proposed different nominees for the leadership. Britain supported a petty chieftan named Abbas Kupi, leader of anti-Communist legalists in Albania (supporters of King Zog) and another friend of Julian Amery. In America the State Department railroaded '...a handful of Albanian refugees in New York into forming a National Committee (for a free Albania) and elected as head a certain Hassan Dusti. Dusti was a young lawyer who, according to OPC, had an impeccable record as a democrat.'[25]

Following this visit, Wisner decided that locations were needed for recruiting and operational planning. Amery chose Italy, containing a large and active SIS station in Rome, and the Americans, Malta. Kupi and his colleagues moved to London and gave a press conference, as they had done in Paris, on behalf of the 'Free Albanian Committee'. Kupi was installed in the Berkeley Hotel, managed by a former member of SOE, and enjoyed a somewhat expensive and luxurious 'safe house'. Shortly afterwards he visited Amery's house in the country, to be questioned by SIS operatives. 'At this point, several people sat down to plan and argue. Amery and McLean had done their work. Planners and operational people were needed now.'[26]

The planned operation was code-named OPERATION VALUABLE. In Washington, the day-to-day control of the operation was in the hands of a Special Policy Committee (SPC). It consisted of four members and represented the State Department, the Foreign Office, OPC and SIS. The State Department appointed Bob Joyce, an OSS veteran with Yugoslavian experience; Lord (Earl) Jellicoe (who five years earlier had commanded SAS troops in Athens) of the British Embassy represented the Foreign Office; Frank Lindsay, head of OPC, and the new CIA/SIS officer, Philby.

There were, however, political problems. For example, before erecting a planned British radio listening post in Corfu, because it was on Greek territory, Greece had to be put in the picture. Only one person could authorize such a potentially sensitive use of Greek facilities, Field Marshal Alexander Papagos, the Greek Army Commander. Via a go-between, Bodosis, a close friend of Papagos, Amery and McLean smoothed things over. Afterwards they discussed the Albanian project with the British Ambassador, Clifford Norton, followed by the SIS Station Chief Pat Whinney, his deputies Eric McLoud and John Baddesley. On 25 May, Amery and McLean returned to London and visited various offices to report their progress. They saw Dick Brooman-White and Tommy Last at SIS HQ, Anthony Rumbold and Charles Bateman in the Foreign Office, and Harold Macmillan at the Turf Club.

During this period, the Americans had become more involved, but British and American working methods differed somewhat. Frank Lindsay noted these differences when he wrote:

> I was summoned to a conference in Washington. On entering the room I remarked on an intricate organisational chart on the wall. One of my colleagues – I didn't know he was even interested in the operation, rose and then started his discourse by pointing to the chart and saying: 'I have now worked all this out, and, as you will see, you need 457 bodies for this operation.' He then spoke for forty minutes, without once mentioning the country with which we were concerned. I confined myself to remarking that I didn't think we could find 457 'bodies' and that I would happily settle for six brains. By way of contrast, I went to London a week later and observed the British approach to the same problem. After sitting around a table in a desultory fashion for an hour or two, one Englishman finally said, 'I say, why don't we get old Henry up here? He knows about this.' A day or two later Henry showed up from down in Sussex, and the problem was put to him, he finally agreed to undertake the task, although he said, 'This will wreak havoc with the garden, you know. Just getting it into trim.'[27]

Major Frank Donnelly, a Far East specialist, was attached to

Department Q of SIS. This department was concerned with obtaining, using clandestine methods, all sorts of equipment, arms and explosives for SIS operations. All equipment supplied was free from any markings which, if the operation went wrong, could be traced to Britain. As a Q Department operations officer (basically the quartermaster of SIS) Donnelly was not surprised when in late January 1949, after nearly three years in Q/Ops, he was transferred to the staff of Colonel David Smiley, a former SOE man. Donnelly was told that he was now on special duties and would be working on OPERATION VALUABLE, a combined CIA-SIS venture to land agents on the Albanian coast. (When subsequently involved in the operation in Malta, very few people knew Smiley's real occupation, except for Admiral Power [Naval Intelligence], Major William Major [the Security Service] and Lord Mountbatten.

Smiley had been transferred from the army to SIS. Obviously, a springboard had to be found for the operation. Wisner remarked that: 'Whenever we want to subvert any place, we find that the British own an island.' Including Cyprus, Malta and Corfu. The recruitment of Albanians covered firstly Boston, where certain Albanian collaborators and war criminals lived. They had been denied visas to enter the USA, but subsequently were smuggled into the country by the OPC, placed in charge of the 'National Committee for a Free Albania'. Secondly, POW camps in West Germany also contained the same sort of Albanians who could be recruited. Once employed, they were moved to a special school near Berchtesgaden to be trained by Colonel Brian Franks of the SAS.

Soon the operation began. Safe houses were found in Greece by C. M. Woodhouse, who had served with Amery in Albania. Smiley and a colleague paid a quick visit to Athens to discuss with the CIA representative, and head of the British Military Mission the possibility of using Corfu as a springboard for the operation. Smiley additionally visited Malta and saw Michael Burke of the CIA (OPC men Kermit Roosevelt and Richard Bissell had earlier approved Lindsay's choice of Burke who had served with the OSS in France and the Balkans) and Major William Major.[28] Whilst in Malta, Smiley learned that the Security Liaison Officer (SLO) had been briefed, via the Security Service, to seek army and Colonial Office backing, to find a suitable HQ in Malta which could house 36 men for two or three months; they needed a place where their presence would not arouse local interest or suspicion. Obviously, the area needed to be close to the coast for landing and cliff-climbing exercises, and secure enough for the men to be under control at all times. Smiley told Donnelly that he needed to deal with a supply of small arms, grenades and explosives; that someone was required to train the men in the use of this equipment; and someone was required to train men in wireless telegraphy and attendant codes. Instructions would be required in setting up and running subversive cells, sabotage and guerrilla groups. In addition, money was needed to finance such groups. A boat was also needed to carry the trained agents on the short sea passage to Corfu, an engineer to run it, and a second HQ in Corfu.

In total, Britain provided Malta as a base, the small boats, the training officers, and the equipment. America provided most of the finance and the use of Wheelus Field in Libya as a depot for parachute drops. However, endless discussions took place over communications. SIS at Vienna was asked to help. Stationed there was G. K. Young. He and Donnelly travelled to Malta with a wireless telegraphy officer. There they met the SLO who had also arranged meetings with the army and the Governor's office at which the SIS officer was promised full support and any required military services. The army offered a site called Fort Bingemma, between Rabat and Mgarr, located on an isolated and barren hill. Because the fort was on a high ground, communication with London was easy. Donnelly and Young were able to set up a small aerial at Fort Bingemma, which could transmit and receive messages from London each day. Later Donnelly accepted an offer from the army to make the fort fully ready for working occupation, and he returned to London.

In his office in London, Donnelly met CIA officer Michael Burke for the first time. Burke was using the cover of film executive. Warner Brothers had agreed to release him, investigating Italian and Greek locations. Donnelly and Burke soon set to work to find a suitable boat. They searched the ports of Exeter, Bristol, Brixham, Torquay, Plymouth and Fareham without any success. Fortunately G. K. Young radioed that he had located a possible boat in Malta. So Donnelly returned to Malta with Burke to observe a small, compact motor cruiser, about 45 feet long and powered by a twin diesel engine. It was ideal; the owner, an Englishman, was willing for a quick sale without any questions asked, and accepted £6,000 in cash. Donnelly removed every fitting that could have indicated its origin, and renamed it *Marie Angelo*.

Eventually, a sailor, an elderly man of nearly 70 called Halliday Paterson, was found and flown by SIS on 1 October to Malta where he took over the *Marie Angelo*. Seventeen days later he was flown back again to London, critically ill, and hospitalized at St Thomas's Hospital where he died on 28 October. Paterson's death threatened the entire schedule of OPERATION VALUABLE. G. K. Young once again radioed Donnelly in London informing him that a solution was in hand. Two British brothers, operating out of Malta, had a fast 50 foot motor cruiser and were willing to undertake the job as a package deal and would not only provide the boat, but run it themselves, for a price. SIS engaged their services.[29]

Before OPERATION VALUABLE could enter its operational stage, Donnelly still had two more jobs to do. Firstly, there was the air-freighting of a small rowing boat to Malta, to be used for the taking of the Albanian agents from the motor cruiser to the beach; and secondly, to arrange to pay the agents before they entered Albania. 'After discussions with the CIA it was arranged that the Secret Service [SIS] would provide £10,000 worth of gold sovereigns packed in wooden cases and that the RAF would fly these to Malta.'[30] Donnelly then flew to Athens, and then on to Corfu to join G. K. Young.

Corfu lies opposite Albania. At the nearest point, the two places are approximately three miles apart. Therefore, Corfu was an ideal place to launch the operation. SIS utilized a large villa, the Castello, just west of Castello Bay and Albanian agents arrived by motor cruiser from Malta to be installed there.

Early in December the first six agents, their faces blackened, commando-style, each with his sovereigns in his money belt, packs loaded with weapons and explosives, crossed the channel to Albania. The training agent went along on the cruiser and reported that the men had been landed successfully. Two days later, the operator at the Castello received a signal from the group to say that the agents had made contact with loyalist elements and had been welcomed. All was safe for the other groups to follow as quickly as possible. Four went across without incident, but the fifth was fired on by an Albanian gun-boat. It got safely away in the darkness.[31]

A week passed by without any word from the teams, by which time Young and his W/T operator were gravely alarmed, and were manning the receiver at the Castello on a 24-hour basis. This they continued to do for nearly a month before a message came from the military mission in Athens reporting a rumour from Albania that each and all of the teams had been wiped out or captured within a matter of minutes of landing.

SIS held a post-mortem, and finally decided that the Albanians must have stumbled upon the first team by accident and had then broken the W/T operator, by torture or the promise of his freedom, into revealing the codes and, more important, the duress signal. When the other teams had arrived the Albanians must have been waiting for them.

Philby later explained:

We did finally succeed in landing a small party on the Albanian coast with instructions to work their way inland, spy out the land, and then move southwards into Greece. It was hoped that the information they gathered on the way would help us in launching more ambitious schemes at a later date. The operation, of course, was futile from the beginning. Our infiltrators could only achieve something by penetrating the towns under Communist control... It was clear, at least, that they had nowhere found arms open to welcome them.[32]

(Because Philby had forewarned his centre in Moscow, it was pretty obvious that any infiltrators would be captured first of all, before even discovering any possible open arms.)

However, the operations continued. On 29 April 1950, Enver Hoxha announced that an invasion of mercenaries had been pushed back. One Albanian agent explained:

I parachuted into the Mati in 1950, and soon after Ihsan Toptani, of King's bodyguard, joined me. Others came to join us, some from across the frontier and some by sea. But the ones who came by sea never found us. They landed and the police were always waiting.[33]

But Abbas Kupi, the man that SIS had imposed onto the CIA as the Albanian chief, had, in a training camp, declared to his men:

You are not alone! In Albania there are hundreds of thousands of nationalists in the mountains; the government forces are confined to the towns and cannot go into the countryside; the government has had to proclaim a state of emergency from 10 at night until the morning; some towns are already in nationalist hands![34]

The reality, however, was somewhat different. From 29 May to 6 June the 'trial of air-borne spies in Albania' took place (the spies had been flown in by DC3 planes). The Albanian Minister of the Interior, in January 1951, announced new attempts made by counter-revolutionaries in an unsuccessful infiltration in the north. He reported that 43 émigré Albanians, who had entered the country by parachute and submarine had been defeated by the police in a gun battle lasting several days. In all, 29 guerrillas

51

had been killed and 14 captured. The survivors were tried in October of that year: two were shot, and the remainder jailed.

(Three and a half decades later, the deaths of the men were viewed differently: Smiley, showing his natural compassion and decency, expressed his grief on BBC TV. On the other hand, when asked about the loss of lives, former CIA officer James McCarger observed: 'Too bad!')

The last operation to try and place Albanian counter-revolutionaries took place a few weeks before Easter 1952. At this time, Philby, as a result of suspicions surrounding him over the defection of his friends and co-conspirators, Burgess and Maclean, had been demoted to a field agent, and was no longer privy to information about the Albanian operations, which continued to go wrong.

In order to discover what was going wrong in Albania, Captains Shehu and Sufa, together with a radio operator, were parachuted into the Mati. Once again the police were waiting, this time at the rendezvous point which was a house owned by Shehu's cousin. The police had forced the cousin's radio operator to broadcast an all-clear signal to his SIS base in Cyprus:

> The operator had been schooled to deal with a situation like this. There was a failsafe drill which involved transmitting the signal in a way that warned [that] it was being sent under duress and therefore, should be disregarded. But the militia [police] knew the drill.[35]

This was also known by a pro-Soviet agent at the base in Cyprus. The drill all-clear was broadcast and twelve more agents, including Matjani, were parachuted into an ambush near the town of Elbasan in a place called Saint Gjergji in northern Albania. All were shot and killed by the Albanian Army. Subsequently, Shehu, Sufa and five more were put on trial in Tirana, found guilty, and were shot by a firing squad at Easter. The whole Albanian network was crushed and all the agents shot or jailed.

Most writers have unequivocally blamed Philby for the deaths of countless agents. However, according to one former SOE agent: 'He may have been a scapegoat for the inefficiency of some other people.' Indeed, this was the case. From September 1949, to the late summer of 1951, Philby was in Washington and only knew the broad details. Actual details in terms of dates, times and places of landings came from pro-Soviet sources in Malta, Cyprus and Corfu. 'There must have been a "mole",' explained Colonel Smiley.[36]

In the margin of the Albanian débâcle, here is an extract from a statement made by a British resident in Cyprus, referring to his friendship with an American archaeologist called George McFadden during and just after the final Albanian operation. McFadden had served with the OSS at the end of the war, and had maintained contact with US Security in Cyprus.

In the summer of 1951 he [McFadden] visited me unexpectedly one afternoon. He had learned that I had been a security officer and he probably assumed that I might have some security responsibilities in the organisation[37] for which I was then working. He was suddenly eager, for the first time, to discuss politics. He seemed concerned about the presence in our organisation of pro-Communist and anti-American elements. This interested me because I had reason to believe that some of our employees were Communists and I had tried to interest London [SIS HQ] in the problem, without success. After that we saw each other a little more frequently. He seemed to be interested in the security aspects of recent events in Albania. He thought some kind of leak had occurred through our organisation. He knew a good deal about an Englishman ['G'] belonging to our organisation who had been sent to Corfu during a critical period. He [McFadden] was interested in 'C' [NAME CENSORED], another member of our organisation, who had been in touch with the man in Corfu, and had had a close relationship with a girl who was at one time in Rome and another in Vienna; she had worked for Israeli intelligence but had been fired when it was discovered that she had Communist affiliations.[38]

To the author's knowledge, no case was ever built up against 'Charles' who was corrupt and a drunk. McFadden was drowned in 'mysterious' circumstances ~~~~~ afterwards whilst in the company of 'Charles'. No inquiry was held. 'There was' to quote a former SIS officer 'a [state] cover up.' After all, it would have been most embarrassing for SIS and American intelligence, had it been discovered that an SIS employee had reportedly murdered a former US Security Officer.

5

THE UKRAINE

The CIA and SIS, in addition to wanting to 'roll back' Communism in Albania, also set their sights upon involvement in the Ukraine which was considered to be the greatest objective, right inside the heart of Russia: 'an even more glittering prize.'[1] After all, should Communism not be secure in Russia, the heartland and ideological mentor of Communism, disintegration inside the satellite states was possible, indeed probable.

The Ukraine also had a well-organized and extremely strong resistance movement, both inside and outside the Ukrainian borders, called the Organisation of Ukrainian Nationalists (OUN); its parent and fighting arm was the Ukrayinska Viyskova Orchaniztsiya (UVO). The strength and popularity of the UVO was such that it had been causing internal problems for the Soviet authorities for over twenty years. The UVO had been born out of the unsuccessful war of 1918–20 in which anti-Communist countries were fighting against Russia. During this struggle most of the movement's leaders were captured and imprisoned. One officer, Eyhen Konovalets, fled from Russia 'and took up the nationalist struggle underground',[2] and his organization, UVO, began recruiting from Ukrainian émigrés, including many former soldiers. Subsequently, men were infiltrated back into the Ukraine to set up an internal resistance movement. This resulted in 'a spate of armed attack, political murder and subversion'.[3] In 1927 the UVO merged with other nationalist groups to become the OUN, headed by Konovalets. By 1939 Konovalets was dead. He had been murdered by a Soviet agent who had penetrated OUN and had handed to him a fast-ticking time bomb in a café in Rotterdam.

Following Konovalets's demise, a young Ukrainian, Stepan Bandera, was elected leader of the OUN. Prior to his election, he had escaped from prison when Germany invaded Poland. Bandera took the view that 'OUN should help the Germans drive the Russians out of the Ukraine after which he would set up an independent government'.[4] However, his plans were not realized. The Germans arrested him and later he was banished to a concentration camp at Sachsenhausen. In 1944 he was released after promising to collaborate, but Bandera took a different course and escaped to the West to wait out the remainder of the war. However, prior to the start of war, 'SIS had maintained contact with Stepan Bandera'[5] and SIS considered Bandera to be 'their' man, and so he was. When the Americans came to plan their post-war subversive operations in the Ukraine, they supported Narodno-Trudovoy Soyuz Rossiyskikh Solidaristov (NTS) – which approximately translated means Popular Labour Alliance of Russian Solidarists. NTS was formed in 1930 at a youth a congress in Belgrade, Yugoslavia. It put forward the views of a group of liberal Russian exiles: 'Idealism, nationalism, activism.'[6] Later, NTS developed a more definitive ideological identity which can best be identified with the right-wing of the British Labour Party.

> The ultimate objective of the NTS is to overthrow the Communist regime in Soviet Russia and to replace it by a democratic parliamentary system.[7]

To this end, it had formed, with support, underground movements within Russia. When Germany attacked Russia in 1941 they 'found NTS very co-operative'.[8] NTS hoped for the entire collapse of the Russian regime – assuming that they would then be called upon to run the administration of the occupied territories. Initially things went well. Hundreds of NTS members were employed as journalists on Russian newspapers, teachers, interpreters, and advisers to the (new) German administration. 'But slowly they became disillusioned as they grew to realize that the Nazi aim was to subjugate the Russian people into a state of semi-slavery.'[9] Subsequently, NTS's policy changed from one of co-operation to one of hostility. On the basis of information collected by Admiral Canaris's counter-security services, 62 leading members of NTS were arrested in 1943, and 28 of them were executed. A purge in 1944 put 200 leading members into concentration camps.

At the end of the war, surviving members of NTS, Vladimir Poremsky and Georgi Okolovich, reorganized NTS through the assistance of the Western allies. Finance and facilities were provided by the CIA (published) and SIS (unpublished), in return for intelligence about the Soviet Union and its occupied Eastern Europe. Such information was invaluable to the Western allies. The strict security measures, language difficulties and the Russians' deliberate lack of contact with the people of occupied countries, made Western intelligence work extremely difficult. The Russian members of NTS, trained and experienced in subversive work, were better able to cope, and were the only people who could easily make contact with soldiers and perhaps persuade them to defect to the West. The Western allies were extremely interested in these defectors, not only for political and propaganda reasons, but also for the military information they could provide.

By 1946 NTS members could turn their attention to the hundreds of thousands of Russian military and civilian personnel who were occupying Eastern Europe. They set up NTS groups among the Soviet forces and the Administration, and they not only persuaded but assisted members of the occupied forces to defect. They collected information on the strength and geographical distribution of Soviet forces in occupied territories for the Security Services of the Western allies. They gathered information about the political aims of the Soviet occupying forces during the crucial years when the RIS was successfully establishing itself in one European country after another. During this period, many thousands of ex-Soviet citizens found new homes all over the world. NTS kept in touch with them and organized groups; leaders were appointed in foreign countries and an HQ in Paris was established.

> Now the NTS started to turn its activities towards its basic objectives – the overthrow of the Communist regime in Soviet Russia and the establishment of a free democracy.[10]

Across in Washington, according to Philby, he and the OPC man, Frank Wisner had:

> projects for the penetration and subversion of the Soviet Union itself ... Both SIS and CIA had their Baltic puppets, [SIS had Bandera; CIA had NTS] whose rival ambitions were usually quite irreconcilable. It was with some relish that I [Philby] watched the struggling factions repeatedly fight themselves to a standstill. On one occasion, the position got so dangerous that Harry Carr, the North European expert in Broadway [SIS HQ], was sent to Washington in a desperate bid to stop the rot.[11]

Prior to this, Philby had achieved a major coup by transferring the entire NTS network, on the false grounds of a lack of funding from Britain's impecunious government, to the CIA. Wisner was delighted by Philby's offer, and accepted it on behalf of OPC. Even so, there was not much that the CIA-SIS could offer to OUN-NTS. After all: 'OUN already had clear and relatively swift lines of communication from Germany and Austria, through Czechoslovakia, to the Western part of the Ukraine around Lvov, and they had good supplies and resourceful men.'[12] The CIA and SIS could only offer radio sets, codes, small arms and sometimes, forged documents. The Ukrainians accepted, and joint liaison between OUN-CIA-SIS began. Because Philby was involved everything went wrong. In his words:

A first party, equipped by the British with W/T [wireless telegraph] and other clandestine means of communication, was sent into the Ukraine in 1949, and disappeared.[13]

The CIA-SIS had taken care to ensure that the group was self-supporting: 'equipped and trained to live for long periods without having to depend on any assistance from the local population.'[14] But the precautions did not take into account being 'shopped' by a planner, in this case Philby.

During the following year Philby 'shopped' two more incursions: the high ranking leader, Roman Shukhevych, was killed when he and his team ran into an ambush. His replacement was Colonel Vaselkoval, a cautious and experienced soldier, who failed to report on schedule. The CIA then began to have serious doubts about the usefulness of Bandera to the West, especially in view of the British-sponsored failures.

Philby wrote:

[The CIA's] attack on the alliance between Bandera and SIS gathered strength in 1950, and much of my time in the United States was spent in transmitting acrimonious exchanges between Washington and London on the rival merits of obscure émigré factions.[15]

Eventually a full-scale SIS-CIA conference was held in London in 1951, when SIS refused to jettison Bandera. Later in that year, the British dropped three six-man parties by air (they had taken off from Cyprus). One party was dropped near the head waters of the Prut, not far from Kolomyya; and another was dropped midway between Lvov and Ternopol; and a third party was dropped just inside the borders of Poland, near the source of the San. 'In order to avoid the dangers of overlapping and duplication, the British and Americans exchanged precise information about the timing and geographical co-ordinates of their operations.'[16]

However, the members of the teams were shot or imprisoned. Evidently some changed sides, and 'after a long silence, letters from them appeared in the Ukrainian press. The letters followed a pattern: émigré Ukrainians were Fascist extremists who wished to crush socialist government and substitute capitalist control. They were being helped by Western intelligence agencies which had established training bases in Italy, Austria, West Germany and Scotland.'[17] Even allowing for the propaganda element, the letters were pretty accurate in terms of the involvement of the Western Intelligence Services and training bases.

On 28 May 1954, the Russian government protested to the British government, charging that the British government was allowing NTS to operate in Britain engaged 'in recruitment of persons from among traitors and war criminals, who were being trained and dispatched to the USSR to carry out espionage and diversionist and terrorist activities'.[18] The Soviet charges concerning the recruitment of Ukrainian émigrés were quite correct:

> At the beginning of 1953 [related émigré Tcheresov – not known to be either an ex-Nazi or a war criminal] ... furnished with a passport in the name of a Polish merchant, delivered in West Berlin, I flew to London with Trushnovich and Khandurator. I was seat to a foreign 'university' financed by foreign [Foreign Office] subsidies and directed by the British spy-masters [SIS], to learn how to train the NTS 'solidarists' in sabotage techniques against my people in the Soviet Union. An officer of the British Special Services was waiting for us at the airport, he directed us to a hotel, giving us some money. Next morning we were driven to a building near the Aviation Museum. It was the espionage school. The building also contained several military offices. You could only get in with a permit. The courses lasted three weeks. The British instructors taught us the rules a spy should follow from the moment he touches foreign soil, methods of military, economic, scientific and technical espionage, subversion against the Communist and workers parties and the people who participated in them. All things which had been drawn from English and American experience.[19]

With regard to the Soviet charges that NTS (and SIS) were recruiting war criminals, the charges were quite correct. But both organizations did so for totally different reasons. SIS certainly were not adverse to recruiting any type of Ukrainian émigré be he an ex-Nazi, a war criminal, or a prominent collaborator for their counter-revolutionary operations.

The NTS, however, deliberately chose men who had been involved in Jewish atrocities. Eventually they found themselves going into the Ukraine to be shot or imprisoned. Those who escaped such a fate somehow 'mysteriously' and secretly 'disappeared', much to the liking of world-wide Jewish communities and the Mossad. The latter organization may have been involved, they certainly approved.

Bandera (in a letter from the Assistant Chief of Staff, USAF, European Theatre, dated July, in reply to a request for the apprehension of Bandera, from General Sidlov, Chief Soviet MKVD, Brandenburg, Germany, dated 29 June 1946) was described as a 'war criminal', and he still remained free and protected some nine years later. The NTS men, and men belonging to Bandera, formed a large team of infiltrators in 1954 who landed in an isolated region in the Carpathian mountains. As they were walking into the Ukraine, having stopped for a rest, they were ambushed by border police, and the entire unit wiped out. Following this débâcle, the CIA and NTS conducted extensive investigations in order to discover what or who caused the failure. They discovered that information about the operation had been passed from Philby, then (officially) out of SIS, to the Soviets. Philby had gained his information from George Blake (then an RIS agent) who was then working at the Foreign Office in London. Following this discovery, NTS decided 'not to work again with British intelligence [on] further operations'.[20]

RE-ENTER BLAKE

On 1 September 1948, Blake was officially attached to the Far Eastern Department, and knew that in due course, he would be given a posting overseas. The posting turned out to be Seoul, the capital of the Republic of Korea, as vice-consul, to Captain (later Sir) Vyvyan Holt, the British chargé d'affaires. He could hardly have arrived at a more interesting and eventful time. In 1945 the Soviet Union had entered Korea from the north. Similarly, on 8 September 1945, the Americans had landed in South Korea. (Both Washington and Moscow had stated their reason for sending troops into Korea was to enforce the surrender of the Japanese Army which had remained in control of Korea even after the surrender of Japan.) The Soviet and American military commanders reached a temporary agreement with Korea being partitioned along the 38th parallel. The Allied powers pledged themselves to restore, after five years of tutelage, Korea to full independence. However, by May 1946 negotiations with the Soviet Union had broken down. Meanwhile, a civil war was raging in China between the Communist armies of Mao Tse-t'ung and the Nationalists of Generalissimo Chiang Kai-shek. By 1950 the Western intelligence agencies expected a Communist North Korean military incursion into South Korea.

Blake had not as yet become an RIS agent and was at this time, pro-West. However, two traumatic events changed him. Firstly, Germany was being considered to join NATO; and secondly, North Korean troops arrived in Seoul. He reacted strongly to the former, as he took a total exception to allowing Germany to join NATO. One lunchtime, looking out of the windows of the British Embassy in Seoul, Blake observed a long column of motorized American troops leaving (retreating from) the capital. He was astounded; after all, no one at the Embassy had been informed – not even Vyvyan Holt. Blake felt that the West had completely let Holt down, who he had a tremendous love for. As far as Blake was concerned, Holt personified all that Blake aspired to be: a British upper-class and aristocratic country gentleman. Soon an almost father-son relationship of trust and understanding developed between the two men. Holt was what one would call Blake's guru. They discussed politics to a considerable degree. Holt was a confirmed Marxist, and Blake naturally believed when Holt explained to him: 'Marxism is a universal historic inevitability. You ought to join the winning side, George.'[21] These words were kept foremost in

Blake's mind, and, over a period of time, Holt converted him to Marxism.

The incoming troops from North Korea soon took control of Seoul and of the British Embassy there. Several Embassy staff including Blake and Holt were taken by road to Pyong-yang, the Communist capital, 140 miles away, to be interrogated by the North Korean Security Police. A Russian 'apparently an agent of the MKVD, was present'.[22] From there, the team of captives, including Holt and Blake, undertook a journey by train which lasted six days and six nights. Their destination was a POW camp at the town of Man-po on the river Yalu, near the Manchurian frontier. They arrived on 11 September 1950. A month later the POWs were made to commence what turned out to be a death march. During this forced march, Blake tried to escape to find American tank patrols who were rumoured to be nearby. He was not successful and was recaptured. Eventually, by 8 November the POWs arrived at their destination, the village of Chung-Kang-Djin. 'Commissioner Lord, helped by George Blake and Philip Deane [correspondent for the London Observer] made a rough estimate of the casualties. They found that at least a hundred people had died or had been shot during the march.'[23]

During January the following year there was 12 degrees of frost, but the prisoners' ration of firewood was never enough to warm their thin-walled huts. Blake suffered from prolonged bouts of dysentery, influenza as well as severe frostbite. Holt fell very ill: indeed he was expected to die. However, Blake nursed him through this illness. Because Holt was no longer able to read, Blake read to him. But only Marxist books were available. As a result, the two discussed politics for hours and Holt re-emphasized that Marxism was going to become a historical inevitability, and again urged Blake 'to join the winning side'. It was only now that Blake became a Marxist, in line with his friend and mentor, Holt, and it was not, as has been widely believed, at the hands of his Korean guards. According to Gregory Kuzmitch, Blake's interrogator, who defected to the

63

West, firstly, Blake had revealed very little about either his work as vice-consul or as an SIS officer in Seoul. Secondly, Blake did not give any information about his SIS training or about SIS which might have been of use to the Communists at that time And lastly, despite Blake showing a deep disillusionment about Western politics, being very critical of the American and United Nations intervention in Korea, even more so of Britain's support of this action, he had not shown signs of being willing to become a convert to Communism. Kuzmitch gained the impression that Blake was a 'sympathizer' and good material to be 'turned round' to the Communist cause.

At Blake's trial, the Attorney-General told the court that 'Blake's political and philosophical views underwent a change in 1951'. Blake himself stated in his confession that he had come to the conclusion that the Communist system was preferable to Western capitalism. At this time in Korea, he had not wished to become a Soviet agent. However, this situation changed when, following release from captivity in early 1953, he travelled by train across Siberia to Moscow. Blake is somewhat reticent about this period. He has only gone as far as to say (to a mutual friend) that it was here in Russia where he was recruited to become a Soviet agent. Reading between the lines, Blake implied that perhaps he had been blackmailed into doing so (possibly as a result of tapes held by the MKVD covering his quasi-homosexual relationship and conversations with Holt). By the time he arrived back in England, he was a Soviet agent. Philby was somehow informed. Blake and Philby met, once again, this time both as Soviet agents. This relationship was a very deadly one indeed especially in connection with the ill-fated 1954 Ukraine operations. But as we shall see later, these two worked together once again in Beirut in the late 1950s and early 1960s.

6

A DOWNFALL – AND IRAN

Midway through the Ukraine operations, Philby (in 1952) found himself returning to London from America under a cloud of suspicion following the defection of Burgess and Maclean to Moscow. American pressure resulted in Philby losing his SIS position. However, despite being demoted, he became a field agent. In this role he spent a few months in Iraq, a period of time in Jordan, and was sent in the guise of a geological explorer to Turkey.

The fraternity of CIA officers in the Middle East included many of Philby's good friends, such as Miles Copeland, with whom Philby had frequent political discussions, Kermit Roosevelt, who was responsible for CIA operations in the Middle East, and Wilbur Crane Eveland, who helped execute many of the CIA operations. As a consequence, Philby learned about operation AJAX.[1] The plan was to stage a coup in Iran by generals loyal to the Shah. Philby hurried back to London with a plan of his own which he hoped would restore his former SIS position. His plan was to enlist and secure the assistance of Iran's Minister of the Interior, General Fazollah Zahedi, who was supported by the army and, according to Philby, the General was willing to depose Prime Minister Mossadeq. When Philby eventually submitted the plan in London to Major-General Sir John Sinclair, the Chief of SIS (1951–56), his plan was met with 'an unenthusiastic response'.[2] But despite this, the plan was adopted.

At the end of World War II, the director of Britain's new Joint Intelligence Bureau, Sir Kenneth Strong, visited Washington in 1946, and had extensive talks with General Eisenhower on plans for intelligence co-operation with America. This was the start of what was to become a 'special relationship' which manifested itself in numerous parts of the world, including Iran in the early 1950s.

Iran had become dependent on its oil wealth extracted by the British Anglo-Iranian Oil Company (AIOC) now BP. Fifty-one per cent of AIOC's shares were owned by the British government.[3] (The shares had been purchased for £2,200,000 in 1914.) Between 1915 and 1950, AIOC realized a profit of $613 million; the Iranian government realized only $316 million.[4] The unequal proportionment of such dealings helped fuel a nationalistic upsurge in Iran. In 1951 Dr Mohammed Mossadeq, leader of the newly-formed nationalist coalition party, the National Front, swept into power. As Prime Minister, he immediately presented a bill to Parliament for the nationalization of AIOC. The bill was passed unanimously, and the young Shah signed it even though he earlier had opposed it, and it became law. The British government was dumbfounded. The *Daily Express* headlined this situation: 'Mossie Grabs Britain's Oil – But Navy to the Rescue'. Secretly, the British government were preparing a plan for the invasion of Iran, called OPERATION BUCCANEER. In the meantime, SIS officer, Montague Woodhouse, second son of the 3rd Baron Terrington, had arrived in Iran.

Woodhouse took the view that:

The Communists' efforts had so far been directed at expansion in Europe and the Far East, [and] it was not hard to guess that the next problem would be in the Middle East. The weakest spot seemed to be Iran.[5]

Iran contained the Tudeh or People's party, one of the largest

Communist-controlled parties outside of the Soviet bloc. In addition, there was the strong anti-British feeling over the Anglo-Iranian concession, coupled with a virtually ineffectual Shah as ruler of Iran.

In response to the Iranian government's action the AIOC organized a world-wide boycott of Iranian oil. This boycott caused a serious financial problem for Iran. Riots broke out in Iran, described by Mossadeq as 'the natural reaction of the people to generations of looting by the British'.[6] The British government responded by evacuating all British women and children on board HMS *Mauritius*, code-named OPERATION MIDGET.[7] Concurrently, a parachute regiment was dispatched to Cyprus on an emergency stand-by. British troops stationed in Iraq also went on alert. By September 1952, Mossadeq served notice on all British AIOC employees to leave Iran and instructed Iranian troops to occupy the oil refinery in Abadan. Britain, once again, sent in HMS *Mauritius* to join smaller ships off the Iranian coast with a view to shelling Abadan. Woodhouse, and 'the Brothers', Seyfollah, Qodratollah and Affadollah Rasidian, combined together, could in Woodhouse's opinion: 'influence opinion in the Majlis [Parliament] and the bazaars and more important, they could mobilize mobs, which were a powerful force in Tehran.'[8] 'The Brothers', funded by Sam Fall at the British Embassy in Tehran, acted as British agents in Iran, dispersing bribes to officials and politicians and paying for strongarm men and hired mobs.

At this point, as part of a destabilization operation, SIS planned the opening of a radio station in Cyprus, (similar to the SIS offshoot, the Near East Arab Broadcasting Station) due to target broadcasts into Iran. However, owing, it is believed, to American pressure, the operation had to be aborted. Such a move was not liked in certain quarters – especially by one man, who had been recruited in Britain (he had sold his house) and found himself in Cyprus without a job.

By October 1952, the British Embassy in Tehran was closed and its staff returned to London. However, in the meantime, nine months after it had been nationalized, AIOC approached the British government proposing the toppling of Mossadeq and oil de-nationalization, under an operation to be subsequently code-named BOOT by SIS. SIS had come to the conclusion that help would be required from the CIA. Therefore, in America, Woodhouse had talks with Bedell Smith over the type of regime they wanted to replace Mossadeq, and its possible ruler. Woodhouse also found Frank Wisner, then the Director of Operations, very useful indeed. During this period SIS was still paying the Rasidian brothers £10,000 a month.

When the CIA officer, Kermit Roosevelt, passed through London in November 1952, he was approached by AIOC, and subsequently he met the operating elements of SIS, General John Sinclair, the Chief of SIS and his future Vice-Chief, George Kennedy Young. It was explained to Roosevelt that what SIS had in mind was the overthrow of Mossadeq. 'They wanted to start immediately,' Roosevelt subsequently recorded.[9]

SIS officials then journeyed to Washington to urge the US government to adopt a detailed plan. At these meetings G. K. Young persuaded the CIA to take over the SIS plan.[10] The CIA renamed the plan as operation AJAX. In February 1953, a British delegation, including General Sinclair, went to Washington for a series of formal planning meetings which CIA Director Allen Dulles attended. Dulles supported AJAX, and plans were laid with SIS as 'the driving force'.[11]

On 18 March, SIS HQ London received a message from Wisner that the 'CIA was ready ... for the overthrow of Mossadeq. It was confirmed in mid-April by a further message from Washington on the authority of Bedell Smith.'[12] Within three weeks, the Prime Minister, Winston Churchill, who was briefed from time to time by Woodhouse and knew of his 'personal involvement in the operation',[13] sanctioned the operation.

Now it was time to act: CIA and SIS officers and agents were in place in Iran. The US still had, a military mission attached to the Iranian Army, 'and its members were in close touch with their Iranian conferers'.[14] American staff at the US Embassy,

Tehran, were also increased.[15] And British officers including Arthur Temple Franks[16] (who subsequently became the Chief of SIS), were said to have 'very close relations with the Palace'.[17] SIS had also established highly clandestine communication channels for the CIA and the principal SIS collaborators via SIS in Cyprus;[18] and this was organized by G. K. Young.

The Iranian police force had been the most successful area of infiltration by US agents. Aware of the pro-US elements in the police, Mossadeq's newly-appointed police chief, General Ashuf Tus, gave orders to dismiss them. However, on 19 April, Tus was kidnapped and killed by undercover SIS agents,[19] as part of OPERATION BOOT.

US General Norman Schwartzkopf travelled to Iran to see some of his 'friends'. They included General Hassan Afra, a bitter opponent of Mossadeq, who had a well-trained private army on his estate in Larak outside Tehran. Another friend was Fazollah Zahedi,[20] described as 'just the man one would choose to set up a coup' (a view with which Philby fully concurred). Zahedi was ruthless and enjoyed manipulating people. It was not clear whether the Shah would co-operate with OPERATION AJAX. G. K. Young arranged a meeting between US Army Lieutenant-Colonel Stephen Meade and the Shah's twin sister, Ashraf, who had a great influence over her brother. Meade was to inform her that Kermit Roosevelt was about to go to Iran.

Having slipped across the Iranian border on 19 July, Kermit Roosevelt had an audience with the Shah at the palace. They agreed that Mossadeq should be replaced by General Zahedi – and Roosevelt reported this back to G. K. Young in Cyprus. The Shah and Roosevelt were, concerned about Mossadeq's plan to abolish the parliament he described as 'a nest of thieves'. Mossadeq had also asked for power to deal with the 'sinister elements in the army, the police, and with other brainless agents of international reaction.'[21] The latter phrase was a thinly-veiled reference to the Shah, and he then decided 'to call a halt' and issue a decree for Mossadeq's dismissal.

The Shah entrusted to General Nassiri the task of serving Mossadeq with the decree of dismissal, proposed and written by the CIA. However, Nassiri, when he arrived at Mossadeq's residence, was flung into jail. Mossadeq announced over the radio that he had refused to obey the royal decree. Another decree from the Shah appointed Zahedi as Prime Minister. The following day, because of massive anti-Shah demonstrations in Tehran, the US Ambassador suggested that the Shah leave Iran. The Shah agreed, and flew to Switzerland.

Meanwhile in Iran, huge amounts of new American equipment had been distributed,[22] thus providing a psychological and morale boost to the pro-Shah elements in the armed forces and elsewhere. A civil war threatened to erupt. On the one side was the widely supported Mossadeq, and on the other side were pro-Shah elements in the police and the army, together with landowners. The latter were backed by the CIA and SIS, and also AIOC. CIA officers included: Howard Edward 'Rocky' Stone, who had 'a reputation as one of the Agency's best coup engineers';[23] Donald Dowes; and George Carroll, a friend of General Farhat Dadsetan, Zahedi's first military governor of Tehran. Carroll candidly claimed 'the organization of gangs, armed with clubs, knives and stones, and occasionally a pistol or rifle.'[24] Roosevelt's agents were ready to bribe various 'merchants' into action.

Then on 13 August, the attack was launched: crowds of 'merchants' armed with staffs and daggers, picks and bicycle chains suddenly emerged from the direction of General Afra's estate at the southern entrance to Tehran.[25] Crowds of prostitutes, musicians, wrestlers, tumblers, jugglers and weight lifters, all of whom had been paid three, dollars each by the American-financed Patriotic League 'led by a right-wing bazaar leader named Shanban Jaafari'[26] swarmed up into Parliament Square, to be joined by army and police NCOs. Suddenly thousands of anti-Mossadeq leaflets appeared. As spectators grew in number, the bizarre assortment of performers began shouting pro-Shah slogans in unison. By this time, the crowd were deliriously chanting 'Shah! Shah! Long live the Shah!' and 'Death to the traitor Mossadeq!' and in one precarious moment, the balance of public psychology swung against Mossadeq.[27] Then the army, led by Colonel Timor Bakhtiar, marched into Tehran, Mossadeq was deposed, arrested and imprisoned by Zahedi, and the Shah was restored as ruler of Iran.

Britain subsequently was paid a heavy compensation for the nationalization, and AIOC (now BP) received a forty per cent share in the oil fields. The balance of the shares was put in the hands of American and continental companies.

The joint SIS-CIA operation had been missed by Philby, but his prediction that General Zahedi would become the new pro-Western premier restored his reputation with the Russians. Even in London a flash of reflected glory shone briefly on him.

7

THE MIDDLE EAST

The influence of Kim Philby and his ideological allies and dupes on British policy and actions in the Middle East, has generally been underestimated mainly because he was overtly concerned with the region for a relatively short period. His real interest in it, particularly in the Levant, Cyprus, Turkey and the approaches to the Gulf of Suez, was keener and covered a longer period than most observers have realized Even when he was running the Soviet Section at SIS HQ, he briefed himself on the politics of the Near East and SIS activities there. Philby did not control a Communist network or faction, but he recruited and influenced the placement of more than one hundred employees of the SIS and its offshoots, several of whom were posted to the Near East. His pro-Soviet task was facilitated, often unwittingly, by many people in and around Whitehall and SIS HQ. While Philby, Blake and other major Anglo-Soviet spies were inflicting shark-wounds on the West, several smaller fish were quietly nibbling away in the British FO and SIS, in covert propaganda services, and the media. Some of them had been influenced by Marxism during the depression or World War II, and had prudently drifted away from left-wing involvements, but for the most part, they remained sentimentally pro-Russian without becoming Soviet agents. Some of this number were younger people who, like most members of diplomatic, security, police and other

72

strongly hierachized services, studied their bosses' prejudices, inhaled the departmental atmosphere, and adjusted their opinions accordingly. Most were anti-American because of McCarthy, Korea or simply envy of America's vitality and wealth.

As Ray Alan has written:

> The fashionable guru in and around Whitehall was Arnold Toynbee, although few there had really read him. Philby and his allies, and individuals with a similar outlook, did more to condition the 'intellectual' atmosphere in sections and offshoots of the SIS and FO concerned with the Near East in the late 1940s, 50s and 60s. These units were all compact enough for a few determined men to influence them with similar ideas, attitudes and clichés. The upper echelons of the FO and SIS were smaller than they are today: everyone knew everyone else, and there were fewer compartments. 'Philbyite' influence even persuaded Mid East specialists in the FO to exploit diplomacy in a dialectical, almost Stalinist manner, subordinating it to propagandist opportunism, for example, or exploiting it to discredit the few democratic parties that sought a middle way between disintegrating traditionalism and extremism of right and left.[1]

Philby, and those who thought like him, were also helped by the relative autonomy their services enjoyed. Both Labour and Conservative governments allowed them a free hand. Ministers nominally responsible for the secret services, from Bevin on, did not know what these services were doing, but covered up for them, if necessary, by lying in the House of Commons![2] Most of the men in London responsible for what passed as British policy in the Near East – officials and their nominal political bosses alike – were ignorant of Near Eastern affairs in those countries, as described in John Kimche's *Both Sides of the Hill*. And the men they posted to the region were not always better informed. For example, of the half-dozen or so British officials who ran a major SIS propaganda operation in the Arab states for ten years after 1946, intervening continuously in Arab politics and trying to influence the Arab media, only one man had first-hand experience of Arab affairs, and he moved on to other duties after four years. (The senior News Editor of the same organization, the Near East Arab Broadcasting Station, boasted that he sold, to SIS HQ, reports supposedly originating from a highly-placed Arab source which were in fact written by a member of his Arab staff with whom he shared the proceeds. The Arab drew heavily on magazine articles. One 'major' report was lifted almost entirely from a mass-circulation American magazine but nobody in SIS HQ appeared to notice.)

British actions were not always co-ordinated with declared British policy and sometimes opposed it. Government policy was often so vague and ill-formulated that it left a vacuum which Philby's followers and other anti-Western people could easily fill. Some offshoots of the FO and SIS became bases for activity and propaganda that sniped at the United States and other Western countries, discredited successive British governments and, directly or indirectly, helped the Soviet Union and its allies in the region. A British disinformation service, broadcast to Egypt in 1956 at a time Britain was still heavily dependent on American support, economic and military:

> To Egyptians, the United States is a totally imperialist country populated by mean and cowardly people who terrorise the weak.

Another specimen of disinformation from a BBC World Service commentary (an FO-inspired editorial) in 1969, was:

> If Saudi Arabia is sincere in its support of the Arab cause it should begin by casting off its special relationship with the United States of America.

Both the Near East Arab Broadcasting Station (NEABS) and the Arab News Agency (ANA), were SIS-controlled, financed by the

74

British Treasury. The two media organizations incited the Arabs to attack Israel. In 1948 NEABS and the ANA helped create the Arab refugee problem by broadcasting a communique attributed to Azzam Pasha, Secretary-General of the Arab League. The communique urged that the Palestinian Arabs should leave their villages 'so as to make way for the glorious armies'. (Azzam later denied having issued this call.) The Egyptian government, quoting broadcasts, from NEABS, accused Britain in the mid-1950s of trying to 'sow confusion and despair among the Arabs and sidetrack their struggle for liberation'. Informed Arabs, Americans, Israelis and Europeans spoke with rare unanimity of 'English perfidy'. But then the interests being harmed were mainly British; as a glance at a few of the activities financed by British officialdom will reveal.

The Near East Association (NEA) was registered in Cyprus in 1950. It was able to 'promote the exchange of cultural and general information throughout the Near East' by broadcasting, publishing and other means without having to reveal any details of its membership, resources or financial activities. The NEA was, according to the *Sunday Mail* of Nicosia,[3] 'the first and only association registered under the Companies Limited by Guarantee Law of 1949'. One suspects that the law was promulgated by the British colonial administration in Cyprus (which did not then have a parliament) in order to enable the NEA to operate. The nominal directors of the NEA were respectable front men who appear to have had no influence over policy and operations. The NEA played a part in keeping the Arab-Israeli pot boiling, and thereby stimulated British arms exports to the Middle East until Russia and the United States took over most of that trade: but now it is remembered chiefly for its connection with the murder of Britain's only Moslem ally, King Abdullah of Jordan.

King Abdullah owed everything to Whitehall, his created

kingdom, his British-commanded army and his income, and although considered a traitor by most politically-minded Arabs, he was a moderating factor in the Arab imbroglio. He was shot and killed by a member of a Palestinian family famous for its hostility to Britain (its head, a decade earlier, had been a pro-Nazi Moslem leader). Although the murderer, Musa el-Husseini, was known to be anti-British, a British official of the NEA had appointed him the association's representative and correspondent in Jordan, a post which gave him access to Abdullah's court. After Abdullah's murder, Husseini and five accomplices were executed. Two of Husseini's associates left Jordan for Cyprus where they contacted the NEA office in Limassol.

The NEA was, in theory, responsible for the output of the Near East Arab Broadcasting Station (known in Arabic as Sharq el-Adna). The station's main studios and transmitters were at Jaffa, near Tel Aviv, until 1947, then they were moved to Limassol in Cyprus. The station seemed destined to be the target of attacks from other British institutions. British members of the Palestinian Police shot up one of its cars for failing to halt (the occupants of the car, described by the policemen as 'suspicious-looking characters', were British security men). The British administration in Cyprus protested to the Colonial Office, for onward transmission to the Foreign Office, about the drunkenness and improper behaviour of some of NEAB's senior British staff. Members of the House of Commons grumbled that it was indulging in political mischief-making, only to be assured by the Foreign Secretary, Ernest Bevin, that it was not under official control. Finally a British military unit occupied it to put an end to allegedly treasonable activity.

One important NEABS section was run for years by an Arab Communist writer who later edited a leading pro-Soviet newspaper. Some other members of its Arab staff later made revelations that indicated they held anti-British sympathies: a few had been in contact with anti-British Arab and Cypriot extremists. A newly-arrived British director of NEABS asked his senior commentator: 'What line do you take on something unexpected if there's no guidance from London?' To which the commentator replied: 'If in doubt, my inclination is to follow the *Economist*.' The director gasped and claimed: 'Heavens! My preference is for the *New Statesman*.' On two occasions, when controversial broadcasts by NEABS and doubts about its ownership caused unease at Westminster, the *New Statesman* defended the station. In its last three years, NEABS broadcast commercials in order to create the impression that it was privately owned. During the Suez crisis, the same director, a left-wing oddball whose previous post had been in Moscow, endangered the lives of British and French servicemen and security officers by allowing his staff to broadcast a warning of Anglo-French invasion plans. It was this act that led the British army to occupy the radio station. Old Mid-East hands used to tell of battles in the 1920s and 30s between Arab tribes subsidized by rival sections of the British Foreign Office and the now disbanded Colonial Office. Here in 1956, was a British military action against a British SIS outpost!

The Arab News Agency (ANA) was not part of NEA's nebulous empire, although, like NEABS, it had been founded during the World War as a propagandist instrument. (Because Britain was the predominant colonial power in the Middle East and southern Asia, anti-British feeling was widespread in the region and even educated Arabs had tended in 1940 to look to Berlin for 'liberation'.) After the war, NEABS and ANA continued to be financed and controlled by British officialdom, but Arab journalists and their readers were encouraged to believe that the ANA was linked with the newly-formed Arab League. Its head office, like the HQ of the Arab League, was in Cairo.

To appease the Egyptian censorship and avoid being closed down, the ANA had to devote space in its news service to extreme Islamic and Arab-nationalist positions. Even more than NEABS (which operated from a British colony whose administration had been told not to interfere with it), ANA became the prisoner of its own propaganda, entangled in its own camouflage. When there were skirmishes between India and Pakistan, ANA had to be anti-Indian, thus heightening Indian mistrust of Britain. When Egyptian and Iraqi politicians campaigned for the expulsion of British troops and political influence from their countries, ANA had to climb on the bandwagon. It had to give prominence to speeches and editorials inciting the Arabs to attack the Israelis, the Kurds and the French, and denigrating the Americans.

Apparently, none of the officials in London responsible for the ANA operation knew that newspapers and news agencies were censored in every Arab state except Lebanon. Incredibly, no one had realized that ANA would inevitably become the hostage of whoever ruled Cairo. Soon, despite Britain's severe economic difficulties and inadequate investmeant at home, British taxpayers were financing a news agency whose output contained a startling number of stories hostile to British and other Western interests. Arab nationalist and Communist newspapers spiked ANA's odd pro-British item but used its anti-Western material gleefully. ANA was not only anti-Western but it was free, although to shore up the 'commercial' front, token bills were sent to the main newspapers and radio stations that took the ANA service. Communist papers in Europe also published ANA items. Reuters, the only British news agency with international standing, was harmed by association, having been persuaded by Whitehall to allow ANA to distribute its material. Some of the rot even spread to the BBC and Fleet Street where commentators and editors received ANA material and, not knowing that it was a propagandist product slanted to suit the whims of Arab politicians and censors, sometimes used it as the basis for comment on the Middle East scene.

A British official who went on an opinion-gathering tour of North Africa in the 1950s heard complaints from British diplomats about the anti-Western tone of much ANA material. At the end of his tour he referred to these complaints in his report. A few weeks later he came under heavy pressure from SIS HQ requiring him to identify the diplomats. On another occasion, when an official protested at SIS HQ about the anti-Western output of ANA, he was told: 'But it's marvellous cover!' Official cover had become unofficial cover for Western, in particular British, interests.

Fuller details of the activities of the organizations mentioned here would only divert us from our Philby theme. But as an indication of morale in which one former SIS official has called 'this fetid, cynical sector of British officialdom' in the mid-1950s, here is an extract from a letter written by a middle-grade British official in what might have been called Philbyland to a colleague ('Broadway' means SIS HQ):

> You would be most unwise to [say anything about this] through local or Broadway channels – you know for yourself how rotten this organisation is – and X is quite frankly here for a quiet life, much as he despises Y. It's a miracle no Broadway heads have fallen already after all that has happened and having survived so much they're not likely to give themselves away at long last by admitting something.[4]

This was the kind of atmosphere that Philby and his fellow sharks had produced and, for a few years at least, it flourished. In September 1956 he was posted to Beirut. Shortly before his arrival the British Foreign Secretary, Selwyn Lloyd, had expressed his concern to improve security and stability in the

Middle East. The Beirut station of SIS had been enlarged, and SIS men John Edes and George Blake were extending their contacts in the Levant. Philby, arrived in an ideally 'conditioned' situation. The Middle East had become a theatre of the cold war. The Soviet Union was making overtures to nationalist movements and the new governments of former colonial or Western-dominated states.

Egypt, Syria and Iraq were all receiving Soviet attention. The US government formulated the Eisenhower Doctrine which allowed the use of American forces, if necessary, to resist Communist aggression against any nation in the Middle East which sought help in meeting an attack. The Doctrine was approved by the US House of Representatives,[5] in January 1957. The main Soviet threat to the Middle East, and then via the Middle East to the West, was not of a military nature, but more of a political and economic one, and was exercised not directly but by proxy. In Kim Philby, Moscow had an able, well-informed and ruthless ally.

This chapter has been graphic in terms of describing events in certain SIS units, and is not an attack against SIS, widely regarded as one of the best intelligence services in the world. Instead, it shows the effect of what Communists, pro-Communists and assorted left-wingers did to SIS in an area which had become (in the words of former SIS officers) 'Middle East Philbyland'.

8

THE SPY WHO RETURNED FROM THE COLD

By 1956 Philby was back in an official role for SIS. Sir John Sinclair, the Chief of SIS (1951–56) and his Vice-Chief, George Kennedy Young, wanted Philby back in the field, ostensibly as a journalist. And this they arranged. A discreet approach was made to the editor of the *Observer*,[1] David Astor, who according to a former CIA official was made cognizant of Philby's SIS role. Accordingly, via a joint arrangement with Donald Tyerman, the Editor of *The Economist*, it was agreed to share Philby's services in the Middle East:[2] 'together with the sharing of pay and work ... which gave him [Philby] the position not of a salaried staff member but of a correspondent with a regular retainer plus payments for articles used.'[3]

Philby relished the prospect of permanent employment again as a foreign correspondent, and SIS agent. However, Sinclair insisted that Philby should confine himself only to non-Communist targets.[4] By September he had arrived in Beirut, where he initially stayed with his father[5] in a house called Mahalla Jamil (meaning a beautiful place) in the village of Ajaltun,[6] situated in the hills above Beirut. Next he visited the SIS station in Beirut. The station initially 'ran' Philby without the SIS staff in neighbouring Arab countries being informed. After 12 months of the arrangement working satisfactorily, Philby's position as a contact man and agent-runner was confirmed and he was awarded a larger salary. This new situation was actualized when Young, who was responsible for the Middle East, visited Beirut. The new terms were settled over lunch at the quiet restaurant, The Constable, overlooking the sea.[7] There Philby was told by Young to carry on producing intelligence material for SIS. He gathered the required information, as well as information from agents he employed (when in the position of an agent-runner) who were located in Lebanon.

As soon as he arrived in Beirut he was asking as many questions as possible to all acquaintances and contacts. One of his favourite places for doing this was the Hotel Normandy, on the sea front in Ras Beirut, where Philby had his mail addressed to. The hotel bar soon became his HQ and he visited there every day, when in Beirut, where he was joined by Colonel Slade-Baker, who wrote articles for the *Sunday Times*. The two formed a small nucleus around which other journalists gathered information, stories and gossip for swapping. Philby also attended as many parties as possible in search of contacts and information. Eventually, he became known as a bottom-pincher, suspender-snapper and drunk. As a result of his behaviour, he often passed out at parties owing to drink. After every new outrage his friends would say 'Well, Kim will never be invited again'. But he always was.

Within a month of arriving in Beirut, Philby was dispatching stories to the *Observer*[8] and *The Economist*. His first story was published by the *Observer* on 30 September 1956, and was entitled 'Western Oil Threat by Lebanon'. He continued to send his reports, for the most part, balanced impartial copy. The exceptions were his references to President Abdel Nasser of Egypt. At that time, just prior to the Suez invasion, Abdel Nasser was considered to be Britain's number one enemy. But Philby never considered him to be an be an enemy. In fact, he gained contact and maintained very close links with a group of Arab Nationalists. This group were mostly refugees from Palestine and were centred around Dr Walid Khalidi at the

82

American University of Beirut. As a result of conversations held between themselves and Philby they regarded him as pro-Arab, and hence pro-Nasser.

Egypt was of special interest to Philby (who had visited the country several times) and to Moscow. The Soviet government was indeed pleased with the progress they were achieving in Egypt, and with President Nasser. The Suez invasion had brought the Russian leader Mr Khrushchev and Nasser much closer together. Khrushchev was fascinated by the way in which the Arab nations appeared to be rallying to Egypt's help. In 1956, Khrushchev had considered that he had learnt enough about Nasser to think it worthwhile to gamble on an arms deal, and his appreciation was vindicated. The Suez crisis had resulted in a close economic and political co-operation between Nasser and the Communist bloc.[9]

As a result of the increasing co-operation between Russia and Egypt, the Western media soon described Egypt as being a 'Soviet satellite' with Nasser akin to a Communist. But Nasser was not a Communist and Khrushchev knew that, for in 1957, he said: 'We support Gamal Adel [sic] Nasser although we know he is not a Communist and that he puts Communists in jail in his country.'[10]

When explaining his political position, Nasser said:

I am not a Communist. I am a nationalist. I am a progressive, at least, I think I am progressive. I consider myself a socialist.[11]

On the other hand, SIS certainly did not concur, nor did the British government. In March 1956, British Foreign Minister Selwyn Lloyd set on record that one of the aims of Britain's Middle East policy was to 'dispose of' Abdel Nasser.[12] At a subsequent meeting, CIA officer Wilbur Crane Eveland and SIS officer George Kennedy Young discussed Nasser being 'terminated'.[13] But Eveland did not agree and he thought that he had 'entered a madhouse'.[14]

Notwithstanding American qualms, Whitehall still considered

that there was one solution only, to topple Nasser, by assassination if necessary. Young and officers of the Special Air Service combined together to produce a plan for precisely this purpose. On the other hand, British Prime Minister Eden vetoed the plan. However, he turned a blind eye to an alternative SIS operation which was to be carried out by Egyptian officers. The plan misfired totally when the officers were captured and executed.[15]

In addition to knowing about covert SIS operations aimed against himself, Nasser and the Egyptian Security Services were also aware of the activities of SIS in Egypt. One activity involved the Arab News Agency (ANA) based in Cairo and headed by Tom Little (see the previous chapter). Nasser announced that he was very angry with the extent of SIS penetration in Egypt, and proposed to name all the SIS officers and agents on Cairo Radio.[16] In any event, he did not; but two agents were arrested. One was James Swinburn, aged 51, the office manager for ANA (his position of office manager was a cover provided by ANA) and James Zarb, aged 37, a Maltese businessman. In total, 20 people were arrested including Charles Pittuck of the Marconi Radio Telegraph Company of Egypt, and John Thornton Stanley of the Prudential Assurance Company, both of whom pleaded 'not guilty' during a trial. Captain Mohammed Hefex from Egyptian Security, stated at the trial that the espionage ring had been operating for 14 years, and that in 1953 the Egyptians learned that 'Swinburn was running it ... in permanent contact with SIS man, Oliver Saint John'.[17] Swinburn confessed to his role of running a major SIS network, and was executed; several others were given life sentences. Other 'journalists', including Sefton Delmer of the *Daily Express*, Ann Shapley of the *Evening Standard*, and Eileen Travis, an American citizen working for the *Daily Mail*, were all expelled. The information given by the Egyptian Security Service had originated from George Blake,[18] who had assisted in setting up the network when he had been based in Beirut.' Information concerning the identities of the SIS operatives in Egypt and the main SIS operations, prior to the arrests, had been from when he had been based in Beirut. Information concerning the identities of SIS operatives in Egypt and the main SIS operations, prior to the arrests, had come within the orbit of Philby's knowledge. He was well connected with SIS Cairo. Philby had visited Cairo as the withdrawal of British troops had accelerated, and the responsibility of SIS operations increased. The major SIS operation at that time was the penetration of the Egyptian Security Services. However, across in London at the Ministry of Defence, certain quarters privately expressed their doubts about whether SIS in Egypt was simply 'incompetent',[19] or had the Station Commander, Geoffrey Hinton, a vested interest in confusing the matter? Hinton was a friend of Philby's and both had worked together intermittently, since 1944 Section V days. As SIS Station Commander, he told Philby all he wanted to know; and given his contacts with SIS Cairo, Philby was in a position to discover the identities of SIS operatives in Egypt, plus details of the SIS operations there. Arrests then followed. Egypt and the Soviet Union had gained a major victory, thanks in part to Philby, and also in part to Blake, during 1956.

Egypt and the Soviet Union also gained by Philby's activities and contacts in Cyprus. From late 1951 Philby intermittently worked as a field agent based in Cyprus. During this period he had an office in the British Middle East Office.[20] This organization had been set up by Bevin to co-ordinate military and political thinking 'among the various Embassies and Army HQs which were running Middle Eastern countries when the Allies started to clean up the war'.[21] It was, to quote a Cyprus veteran: 'a little Whitehall in the sun, an umbrella for the lot, all the odds and sods and funnies.'[22] This veteran 'had worked for the British Middle East Office, an offshoot of the Foreign Office. But only for a couple of years. He found its social life too alcoholic and its policies too pro-Communist for his taste'.[23]

At that time, Cyprus contained a considerable Armenian

community. The spiritual and original homeland of the Armenians straddles the political and national borders of the Soviet Union, Syria and Turkey. The Armenians have often suffered from political persecution and massacres, as occurred at Samsun in the early 1920s. Such actions led to Armenians moving to France, Britain, America or the Levant where they maintained a dedicated programme to keep alive their own culture. On the border between the USSR and eastern Turkey, at one time existed the vast kingdom of Armenia. This was the territory that Philby had certainly known about during his days as 'passport officer' based in Istanbul, Turkey. In Cyprus Philby made regular visits to the main Armenian cultural exchange, the Melkonian Institute. There he enthused about the 'set-my-people-free' songs performed by Armenian folk-groups. Additionally, he maintained a friendship with a particular Armenian family, and also had a platonic relationship with a young Armenian girl. His interest was not purely cultural. Just as SIS had planned to have émigrés from the Ukraine and Albania return to form an anti-Communist movement, so they had the same plans for certain Armenian communities. It was Philby's job to gather information and talent-spot likely recruits. It was also his job to inform his Soviet controllers about SIS moves and plans for future operations involving the incursion of Armenian counter-revolutionaries into the USSR via the Syrian and Turkish borders.

Accordingly, Philby visited the border areas in Syria, but in Turkey he was seen by a British scientist. One of the scientists knew Philby slightly, having met him in Cyprus, and asked: 'What on earth are you doing here?' To which Philby coolly replied, 'Collecting geological samples. I'm on holiday.'[24] Once again, the Western plan to use the Armenians in Syria, Lebanon and Cyprus to penetrate the southern USSR was betrayed by Philby, as confirmed to the author by a former SIS officer.

In Cyprus, Philby was observed in Limassol with NEA people, both British and Arab. The Arabs were Palestinians, often anti-British and pro-Communist. Some of whom were employees of the SIS-directed, Treasury financed Near East Arab Broadcasting Station, and, as was Philby, in contact with pro-EOKA guerrillas; the latter received Egyptian money and arms.[25] Later EOKA gave the Egyptians information on British troop movements throughout Cyprus prior to the Suez invasion.

As a field agent Philby took an enormous amount of interest in affecting British policy in the Middle East. Middle East experts have told of the great pressure exerted on post-war policy-makers by the FO and SIS which in turn was influenced by material generated and sent from Philby and his 'friends', who favoured all-out British support of the Arab League. This tied Britain to a fundamentally reactionary group of Sunni-Arab regimes and provoked the hostility of the intellectuals and religious and racial minorities of the region (Kurds, Jews, Copts, Maronites, Mitwali and Ismaili Shiites, Alawites, and others), who had historical reasons for distrusting the Sunni-Arabs. Before long Britain found itself in trouble, with the Iraqi Kurds; the Israeli Jews; and the Alawites who took over in Syria; and the Maronites, Shiites and Druzes who started piling arms in Lebanon. This method of achieving one's aims by pretending to want the opposite and provoking a reaction to it is, of course, standard dialectical Marxist tactics. From some conversations and articles written by experts it is indicated that Philby was a constant advocate of British support for the Arab League.

Syria, on the other hand, turned out to be a disappointment for Russia and Philby, even though both tried very hard indeed to achieve Soviet successes. Syria had become the next country to be embroiled in the East and West theatre of conflict. The West – the CIA and SIS – considered that there was Communist encroachment in Syria, and took note of a substantial arms deal negotiated between both countries.

The CIA and SIS were incensed at such moves. SIS Vice-Chief George Kennedy Young, opined that: 'Syria threatened Britain's survival [and] would have to be subverted or over-thrown.'[26] Soon SIS 'dripped' information into the British media: a front-page article was published by the *Daily Telegraph* (5 May) entitled 'Czech arms for Syria reported; Deliveries said to have begun already' by their diplomatic correspondent. The article was about daily Soviet shipments to Syria. The CIA officer, Wilbur Crane Eveland, knew otherwise, for he had visited Syria's ports without having seen any sign of Russian activity.

Philby, too, knew the true situation, because he had visited Syria many times (when he dispatched stories to the *Observer*), and gained information from Communist and non-Communist sources. He and his activities were observed by the SIS agent Dr E—— A——. Back in Beirut Philby and Eveland discussed Syria – the general consensus among the Western press men, the CIA and SIS was that Syria had 'gone Communist'. However, Eveland did not concur.

Twenty years later in a letter to Eveland, Philby wrote: 'I remember an occasion at the bar of Saint Georges when you argued that Syria (Abdul Hamid Sarraj and Co.) had not gone roaring Commie. I knew that you were quite right but I could hardly tell you how I knew, could I?'[27] No, he could not. After all, his information had come from knowledgeable Communist and/or RIS sources.

Eventually, the Syrians did not turn fully to the Russians, but instead to a fellow Arab state. Syria did not become 'Communist dominated' or a 'Soviet satellite' as prophesied by certain Western intelligence agencies. Just as Philby had been correct as to what would happen in Iran, he was correct as to what had not occurred in Syria.

9

LEBANESE CAPERS

Life in Beirut suited Philby because drinks were cheap. He was invited to many parties and always surrounded himself with SIS and CIA operatives and journalists who all liked 'old Kim'. Moreover, he was receiving three sources of income: from London newspapers, SIS and CIA.

Philby took an interest in Middle East politics, and would spend hours discussing them with a married couple called Yussuf and Rosemary Sayrgh, neither of whom ever suspected him to be an RIS agent.[1] He also took an active interest in Lebanese politics, a scene which nearly ended as a civil war. In this crisis, Philby played a crucial role.

President Chamoun in 1957 endorsed the Eisenhower Doctrine which propounded to contain both Communism and radicalism in the Middle East. The Lebanese President also had an anti-Nasser foreign policy which only aggravated the Christian-Moslem cleavage; and Chamoun proceeded with an electoral reform calculated to reduce the influence of the pro-Nasser sectarian oligarchy. Elections were due to be held in June 1957. Lebanon was divided into four election areas, and the parliament due to be chosen was important because during the following year the parliament would vote for the new president of Lebanon. The US government wanted to see Chamoun re-elected. CIA agent, Zogby, recruited Prime Minister Sami as

Solh, and later was able to add a foreign minister and President Chamoun to his list. Chamoun and Eveland met and agreed that 'funds should be used to support candidates in evenly divided districts where supporting the government's policies'.[2] Prior to, and during, the election period of four weeks, funds were disbursed. Eveland travelled regularly to the presidential palace with a brief-case full of Lebanese pounds and handed them to Chamoun who had 'insisted that he handled each transaction by himself'.[3]

The 'election' resulted in the principal Moslem opponents of the government being soundly defeated, including pro-Nasser Moslem leaders (the Saeb Salaam, the Shiite Ahmad Asad, and the Druze Kamal Jumblatt) and returned pro-Chamoun Moslem deputies with no power base of their own. During the voting, the use of foreign funds by Chamoun and his Prime Minister was so obvious that two pro-government ministers, appointed to observe the polling, resigned halfway through the election period. During the election, there was also large-scale fighting in the north of Lebanon, many were killed and wounded during the voting. Afterwards, bombings and shootings still occurred which in turn led to the US government, on Chamoun's request, to commit $15 million for military and economic aid.

By March 1958, clashes occurred between government forces and rebel bands led by Moslem opposition leaders, including three defeated former prime ministers, and the Druze tribe led by Kamal Jumblatt who was also defeated. On 8 May an anti-government newspaper journalist, Nesbit Metni, was murdered, which again set off a round of violence. In Tripoli the USIS library was ransacked during a riot which left 35 people dead, and 200 more wounded. The anti-government press blamed Chamoun's supposed plan to amend the constitution. By 12 May armed rebellion had erupted in Beirut. Chamoun was called upon by opposition leaders to resign or face a civil war; instead he declared a state of emergency. Outside Beirut, Kamal Jumblatt's army of 2,000 Druze were involved in major fighting. In Beirut, barricades were soon built and bombs continued to explode. The Lebanese army finally repulsed an attack on Beirut, but one-third of Lebanon was now rebel-held. Following the coup in Iraq, Chamoun decided to take action. He handed a document to Eveland, signed (he said) by all members of his government, requesting the landing of US troops under the provisions of the Eisenhower Doctrine and as provided by in Article 51 of the UN Charter. In view of the gravity of the situation, the American government acceded to Chamoun's request, and sent in excess of 10,000 Marines armed with nuclear-capable 'Honest John' rockets. But the main reason for US intervention was in response to the military coup in Baghdad on 14 July which overthrew the monarchy. The US wanted to show a 'strong presence' in the Middle East in order to dissuade, and contain, any revolutionary moves in the area.

The timing of the Iraq coup, evidently, came as a complete surprise to the CIA, even though they quickly claimed 'that Moscow had orchestrated the overall plan [and that] pro-Nasser [Iraqi] officers had plotted it'.[4] However, Sir Humphrey Trevelyan, British Ambassador to Iraq (1958–61), subsequently penned that there was 'no evidence that the coup had direct Egyptian inspiration'.[5] As is to be seen, it had been inspired and planned by members of the Iraqi Communist Party and Iraqi nationalists.

On the day of the coup, Philby was ever-occupied with the historical events in Beirut. Within days of the US Marine landing in Beirut, he travelled to Baghdad to assess the situation in what he would have called the political and military 'balance of class forces' (in true Marxist terminology) and the Communist revolutionary potential.

This chapter has described the events in the Lebanon during 1958 as recorded by journalists and historians. But all have missed one major key variable: a major RIS operation based in Beirut. Philby was deeply involved in the operation which was against the pro-Western states of Iraq and the Lebanon, and the utilization of Jordan as a subsidiary in the operation. The aim of the RIS operation was twofold. Firstly, to involve Western powers in another disastrous Suez situation which would lead to the death of the Eisenhower Doctrine, and the ending of the Baghdad Pact. Secondly, to effect the introduction of pro-Soviet regimes which would sever ties with the West. As to the former, the target was Lebanon and Jordan. By early May a no-win/no-lose situation had emerged between the Lebanese government forces and the rebel factions. The civil war, in the eyes of the Soviets, had to be escalated. Accordingly, on 8 May, the pro-Communist, anti-government newspaper journalist Nesbit Metni was murdered by a party 'arranged by the increasingly active Russians in order to create a rallying point against the government'.[6] The scheme worked because within four days armed rebellion had erupted in Beirut; rebels became entrenched and held the Basta quarter. Philby then went to live in Basta with the rebels, and emerged, from time to time, to provide reports to the press and to SIS Beirut. In fact, Philby provided 'some, if not all, of the materials on which SIS based their reports'.[7] According to the Philby-writers Page, Leitch and Knightley, it was the information from Philby that decided the US government to send the Marines. However, in actual fact, the US government had a more pressing need: 'to establish a beachhead on Lebanese soil in case the Iraqi revolt spread.'[8]

Three days prior to the Marines' arrival, Philby knew and told this fact to his fellow journalists. 'He spoke of a man who knew with certainty what would happen.'[9] In fact, he was the only journalist who knew about the Marines' coming as a result of information gained from an intelligence source. An *Economist* article (not written by Philby) took the view that America had 'marched to the brink of war',[10] and a further article in the same issue claimed that:

The present situation in the Middle East holds out the largest threat to stability in [the] region – and perhaps even to peace in the world – since the war ... the calculated (or miscalculated) gamble of intervention ... is clearly intended to contain and diminish the threat ... not [to] multiply it.[11]

In any event, the Iraqi 'threat' was contained, and the West did not become involved in another Suez disaster. The Russians had hoped for a coup in Baghdad for some time. In fact, elements in the Iraqi army and the Iraqi Communist Party acted in tandem, as they too had been waiting for the opportunity. The major problem for years had been that Prime Minister Nuri Said had allowed only one armed military group to be in Baghdad at any time unless there was a reliable counter-force to pit against the other military group in the event of a coup.[12] But the situation changed in July when a Communist plan utilized Jordan. King Hussein of Jordan, acting upon security reports of an intended Communist Party involved insurrection in Amman, asked Nuri Said for assistance.[13] Said, in accordance with military treaty (known by the Communist Party) agreed and decided to send a brigade headed by Brigadier A. K. Kassem to reinforce King Hussein. Officers close to Kassem kept the Iraqi Communist Party well informed on what was going on, before Kassem moved to Baghdad on 13 July. But two days before, Friday 11 July, Kassem told Kamal Umar Nadhmi, Communist member of the Supreme Committee of the Front of National Union, the precise date of the coup.[14] The Communist Party placed all the party organizers on the alert and simultaneously issued a 'general directive' to the mas'uls of the principal party committees, containing fundamental slogans. The following day, the coup, which involved the Communists, took place.

Philby's known role with regard to Iraq took the form of providing propaganda disinformation. It was a continuous propaganda campaign against those remaining Arab states' governments in the Middle East which had declared themselves to be in normal association with the Western powers and opposed to Communist expansion. This disinformation included 'Suicide Number Three – The Eveland Plan' to turn the Arab states over to Israel, which had been disseminated to Indian correspondents with whom Philby maintained close contacts. The information surfaced in *Blitz*, a left-wing New Delhi newspaper which was often used for attribution purposes by anti-Western newspapers in the Middle East. Following the revolution the Philby-influenced Near East Association gave discreet support to the pro-Soviet Ba'ath parties in Iraq and Syria, in their coverage to Arab recipients; and Philby travelled to Iraq and contributed well-informed articles about the revolution. The slant, if any, was in favour of General Kassem and his revolutionaries. This was not surprising because Kassem in his fight against nationalists, worked in tandem with the Communists. The writer E. H. Cookridge suspected that Philby received inside information from Kassem and from the Iraqi Communist Party.

Receiving information from Communist Party members was standard practice for Philby. He, in turn, according to a former CIA officer 'gave the Russians a steady stream of intelligence from various parts of the Middle East' including, as we have seen, Egypt, Syria, the Lebanon, Iraq and Cyprus in the Near East.

These Middle East chapters have shown that Philby's main value to the RIS was firstly obtaining from a variety of contacts information required by the Soviets. Some of the information was put to a deadly effect, leading to the capture, imprisonment and deaths of Western officers and agents in Egypt. Other information told the RIS what was happening during crucial periods, such as in the Basta quarter during the Lebanese crisis. Some of his reports postulated as to what could happen, in Syria for example. Secondly, Philby was involved in disinformation exercises as mentioned in this chapter. Thirdly, he held an important pivotal position in Cyprus between various organizations, when he was able to effect British policy.

Next we shall examine his role in a coup which had enormous consequences in terms of a Middle East realignment of political and military factors.

10

NORTH YEMEN

Whilst in the Middle East, Philby became involved with as many countries as possible; sometimes countries which were not well known to the West. One such country which drew his attention was North Yemen. 'One of the most isolated and static countries in the world.'[1] For centuries North Yemen had been ruled by a succession of imams (kings).[2]

Between 1904 and 1948, Imam Yaha ruled, to be followed by Imam Ahmed from 1948 to 1962. In 1962 peasants of the Hawhan tribe attacked a group of tax collectors[3] killing three of them. The local army commander wanted to punish the peasants, but Ahmed thought otherwise. Enraged, the officer attacked Ahmed in his castle, and in Taiz a rival, Hamid al-Din Prince Abdullah, proclaimed himself to be the Imam. Rescue for Ahmed came when his son al-Badr rallied the northern tribes and rescued his father. Ahmed was not a person to be ungrateful, and his son soon had a rapid rise in promotion. Since the imam's health was not good, he needed a trustworthy assistant; and al-Badr became the Crown Prince and ambassador for the country holding all the important ministerial posts. He visited Egypt and fell under Abdel Nasser's charm. Politically he considered himself to be progressive. Nasser arranged for al-Badr to visit Moscow and Peking, and persuaded him to have the Russians build a port at Hodeida, send modern arms, and to allow the Chinese to build a road between Hodeida and the capital of Sana. By November, 1955 a friendship pact had been signed between Yemen and Russia. Al-Badr also prompted his father to allow in the country a number of Soviet and Egyptian advisers for a variety of military projects, including military installations on the Red Sea. A Soviet mission arrived in Yemen in January 1957, and a Soviet Legation was opened at Taiz.[4]

In 1959 the, imam fell ill and left for medical care in Rome. During his absence, al-Badr took the opportunity to introduce progressive reforms. When his father returned home to be faced with an uprising in the north and unrest in the south, he set about the situation with his customary ruthlessness. The leaders whom he deemed responsible had their heads chopped off and jails were filled to capacity. A purge was ordered of the liberal reforms, instituted within a month. The country never fully regained its former tranquillity as there were tribal revolts from time to time. During March, 1961, there was an attempted assassination of Ahmed whilst he was in the General Hospital at Hodeida. One officer, Abdullah al-Sallal, subsequently admitted being involved in the attempt.

Al-Sallal and Prince al-Badr had a close relationship. The Prince regarded al-Sallal as a like-minded liberal, and al-Sallal was well established in his confidence. Following the attempted assassination whilst in Hodeida hospital, the imam dismissed al-Sallal, but al-Badr reinstated him and made him Chief of his own guards. Shortly afterwards al-Badr put al-Sallal in charge of Sana airfield. After this he returned to his former position of Harbour Master at Hodeida, and thereafter in charge of the Military Academy at Sana, staffed by Egyptians. 'These different posts gave al-Sallal ample opportunity to contact revolutionaries, gain support from army officers and enlist the technical help of the Egyptians'.[5]

On 18 September, 1962, Imam Ahmed died in his bed and Crown Prince al-Badr proclaimed himself Imam. One of his first moves was to appoint Colonel al-Sallal as Commander-in-Chief of the Royal Guards. As Imam he announced various reform proposals. Many viewed him as being a wishy-washy liberal; 'He was too high on booze, boys and drugs to be effective.'[6] Meanwhile, al-Sallal had obtained permission to bring in some neglected armoured vehicles from Hodeida to Sana. Once they arrived, they surrounded the palace containing al-Badr, and opened fire. When defeat was in sight, al-Badr withdrew and escaped from the palace. Al-Sallal broadcast that Imam al-Badr had been killed, and declared North Yemen to be a republic. Al-Sallal became a Brigadier, President, Premier and Commander-in-Chief of the Republic of North Yemen.

BRITAIN FIGHTS BACK

The news of the coup roused Philby from his continual drinking. He was very pleased indeed to hear the news, and sober, joined a team of journalists who travelled to Sana. The journalists witnessed the populace cheering the new Republican revolutionary regime. Philby joined in the cheering. Later, the journalists, who had travelled to Sana, carried on to Saudi Arabia and met Prince Faisal. The Prince, speaking to Philby, said: 'From what I hear you are not on our side, Mr Philby.'[7] During the next month, Philby again visited North Yemen. He soon showed his support for the revolution and the new regime, when he wrote for *The Economist*, 'It would be a pity if [a bombing incident] results in further delay before Britain decides to recognize that the Yemen revolution has come here to stay.'[8] No doubt his comments and behaviour were not well received by British officials. But the officials would have been further incensed had they known that Philby had somehow been involved in the coup. Philby had been in a position to point out to both Egyptian and Russian intelligence who would be most useful in the event of a coup. He based his observations on his meetings with al-Sallal and other officers in Egypt. Philby would also have pointed out that al-Badr was hardly the sort of man to head a revolutionary regime.

Back in London, the British government did not know what

was going on as they were receiving conflicting reports. Some reports stated that al-Badr was still alive, whilst a following one stated that he was dead.

The American government wanted to recognize the Republican regime and pressed the British government to do the same. 'Many of us in the Government', said Conservative Minister Julian Amery, 'had doubts whether this was good advice. Colonel McLean also had the gravest doubts. There were reports, but they were not all well confirmed, of resistance in the Yemen.'[9] Shortly after the coup McLean met Amery at his residence in Eaton Square, London. They were soon to find themselves once again working together, as they had done before, prior to – in connection with – the joint CIA-SIS operation CLIMBER in Albania, commencing in 1949 (described in chapter 4).

Amery and McLean discussed the situation[10] in Yemen, and eventually McLean decided that he would go to Yemen and assess the situation 'with no support from any official agency and at his own expense'.[11] McLean did not have to dig too deeply into his own pocket, if at all, because he flew by an RAF plane from Northolt[12] to Jordan, where he saw King Hussein. Both were 'old friends'[13] and after their discussions McLean flew (the plane had been held for an hour or so for him, including passengers) to Saudi Arabia to meet King Saud who was 'highly concerned'. From there his journey took him to Aden. Once there, he went to Government House to see the Governor and Commander-in-Chief of Aden, Sir Charles Johnston, and his ADC, Flight Lieutenant Anthony Boyle – all of whom wanted 'Aden to protect its back [from North Yemen].'[14] It was decided that it was best for McLean to spy out the situation in North Yemen. The Sharif of Beihan, Saleh Ibn Hussain, who had been invited to dinner at Government House, interceded[15] and McLean subsequently passed through Beihani territory bordering South Yemen and into North Yemen. He then travelled by truck across East Yemen, up to Najran in Saudi Arabia. When he arrived back in Aden he sent a telegram via Johnston to Amery[16] in London, reporting that 'at least half the country was in Royalist hands and that it would be a disaster if [the government] recognised the Republic'.[17] McLean's report came under the heading of intelligence information.[18]

Upon arriving in London all information for SIS is first filtered to disguise sources and is then passed on in raw form to the relevant section and sometimes to the intelligence group in the Cabinet Office, which processes it before reporting its assessment to the Joint Intelligence Committee (JIC). The assessment of the JIC is reported to the Cabinet's most sensitive committee, the Defence and Overseas Policy Committee. Membership is a closed secret. When asked who attended, Amery replied 'that's secret', but explained that the Defence Committee included the Foreign Office, SIS, Joint Chiefs of Staff, Ministry of Defence members, and the Prime Minister. The PM chairs the Committee which also includes the most senior and trusted members of the other Cabinet and ministerial committees. McLean's information arrived at the Defence Committee just three days before a Cabinet meeting with the recognition of the Republican regime on the agenda. In view of McLean's report, the Defence Committee decided not to recognize the new regime, and likewise advised the Cabinet. The Cabinet's subsequent announcement was not well received by the American government[19] which in December 1962, recognized the Republican regime.

Now certain intelligence organizations took more of an interest: George Kennedy Young, ex-SIS, who had been in charge of the Middle East Section, was approached by the Mossad to find an Englishman acceptable to the Saudis to run a guerrilla war against the Yemeni regime and its Egyptian backers. 'I can find you a Scotsman', replied Young, and over a lunch in the city introduced Colonel McLean to Brigadier Dan Hiram, the Israeli Defence Attaché. The Israelis promised to supply weapons, funds and instructors (who would pass themselves off as Arabs) in the event of any mercenary operation materializing.

McLean journeyed to North Yemen several more times where he saw Imam al-Badr who was certainly not dead. Following one of his visits, the idea of a mercenary operation materialized. Various people and government departments dropped broad hints that something needed to be done. McLean and Amery totally agreed: something needed to be done. Colonel David Stirling and the SIS officer, Nicholas Elliott, also agreed that something needed to be done. That something was a highly clandestine mercenary operation involving ex-servicemen, members of the SAS and SIS operatives. By now the authorities knew about Philby's involvement in the coup, and action had to be taken. McLean canvassed the Cabinet. Not all of the members agreed, with the exception of Julian Amery, Peter Thorneycroft, Hugh Fraser and Duncan Sandys who tacitly sanctioned mercenary involvement. Prime Minister Harold Macmillan fully supported the idea and sanctioned the operation. (Any proposed operation had to be handled on an extremely secret basis, fully shielded from the glare of any investigative publicity. The operation became a classic 'arm's length' operation as there were no 'official' links between the mercenaries and the British government. But the operation could never have been carried out without official support, and the operation became striking in terms of the degree of official connivance and co-operation it managed to acquire.)

McLean and Stirling again met when Stirling suggested the recruitment of ex-SAS men. 'Stirling took on contracts which the government approved, but which it did not want to handle too directly'. Stirling was excited by the idea of the operation: 'the British government still needed his services.'[20]

Next Stirling arranged a lunch with Colonel Brian Franks, an Honorary Colonel of the SAS. (Franks was no stranger to SIS or SIS-linked operations. He was part of OPERATION CLIMBER in Albania where he had trained counter-revolutionaries at a special school near Berchtesgaden in 1949)[21]

Franks recommended Colonel James Johnson, formerly of 22 SAS. In fact, Franks met Johnson at the latter's residence in

Sloane Avenue, Chelsea, one evening and asked him if he would 'organize a mercenary operation in North Yemen' for the Royalists. Johnson agreed,[22] and next met Ahmed al-Shami, the imam's Foreign Minister at dinner in London, al-Shami asked for help and convinced Johnson that he had the necessary funds to mount a cadre of British officers as advisers. The following day Johnson met Abdel el-Wazir, Royalist Minister of the Interior who told Johnson that the priority should be to destroy a force of Soviet MiG aircraft on the southern runway of Sana airport. El-Wazir immediately authorized 'a large expenditure of money'.[23] Thereupon Johnson looked for competent ex-SAS officers. His first choice was Major John Cooper, who as Corporal Cooper had been Stirling's driver during World War II. Cooper had also seen active service in Oman during the Green Mountain revolt. Two other ex-SAS officers were recruited. However, they were short of Arabic-speaking recruits and so Cooper and Johnson flew to Paris to find some. There they met Prince Miguel de Bourbon-Parma, 'a resourceful operator'[24] who found three highly competent French ex-officers for Johnson.

Stirling was also involved in visiting the Middle East and seeing people. On Friday evening, 12 April, at Government House, Aden, he saw Sir Kennedy Trevaskis (who had succeeded Sir Charles Johnston), Sharif Hussain and Boyle. A few days later they all met again to discuss the current situation. Back in London it took Johnson a few weeks to form the first mercenary team of six men. The men, including Cooper, flew from Britain to Bahrain. At the Speedbird Hotel Stirling briefed Cooper.[25] From Bahrain the team flew to Aden and entered without any problems. Officially they should have been stopped at the customs in Aden (or Bahrain) because Duncan Sandys the Commonwealth Secretary had issued a veto, putting a stop on the whole operation. Conveniently, the team were actually in the air before the veto became effective.

According to the *Daily Telegraph* (4 February 1970): 'How

they got past the security in Aden remains a mystery.' There was no mystery. The 'veto' was, in fact, a political PR ploy in order to absolve the government from any political responsibility for the operation. In Aden, the six mercenaries found their movements free from any official hinderance. Government House was used as a 'safe house' courtesy of the Governor's ADC, Boyle. From Aden city they moved to another 'safe house' in Naqub,[26] under the protection of the Sharif of Beihan.

From leaving England at Whitsun, it took the team five weeks to reach the outskirts of Sana when they met Prince Hassan. Cooper suggested the bombing and blowing up of Egyptian planes at Sana airport. Hassan disagreed because 'reprisals could be taken against Royalist families'. Instead, it was agreed that the team would concentrate on weapon training for the Royalist army, and on communications.[27] Cooper returned to London, and saw Johnson on 30 May.[28] A few days later Cooper and Johnson returned to Paris and on 6 June, booked into the Hotel Plaza Athenea, and stayed in the bridal suite.[29] Again they saw Bourbon-Parma about the recruitment of European mercenaries. Such recruits subsequently included ex-French Legionnaires originally born in Russia, Greece, Germany, France and Belgium (some of whom had fought in Algeria). Arab-speaking mercenaries were preferred, but when in Yemen their Algerian accent 'was not fully understood'.[30] Also seen was an Israeli. When asked by the author as to 'what assistance did the Israeli give?' Stirling replied: 'That's secret.' Within a month or so the operation was really under way. Within several months, the operation's cover was 'blown' and was to a minor degree reported in the British media. However, not all of the names of the mercenaries/ operatives were revealed, nor were British government and SIS links disclosed.

On 1 May 1964, the Cairo newspaper *Al-Ahram* published letters said to have been intercepted near the Yemeni border with Beihan state. The letters were between Boyle and Cooper concerning sabotage operations. 'Experience in demolition and small arms', in a letter dated 4 November 1963, from Boyle to Cooper; and dropping arms to Royalists by parachute: 'The arms suppliers would ship direct', in a letter dated 29 November 1963 to Cooper. (The letters were subsequently admitted genuine by a British government spokesman.)

Whilst ADC to Johnston and Trevaskis, Boyle was also an RAF officer and the son of Sir Dermot Boyle. Young Boyle became a Flight Lieutenant before he retired from the RAF in January, 1964. His covert role in the operation put him in a position much suited to SIS. In fact, Boyle had been seconded by SIS to work with Johnson and Stirling. But: 'It was entirely unclear whether he was intended to assist or to provide an official eye to monitor Johnson's activities.'[31] SIS operatives also became involved when 'co-opted to help out with radio monitoring problems'. The Yemen operation 'was the focus of a fierce dispute within [SIS]; many senior officers wanted the government to call a halt to it, but they apparently lost their battle'.[32] The operation continued. Colonel David Smiley arrived in Yemen in June of that year with McLean (Smiley was contacted by McLean in May) ostensibly as a journalist. He had been invited by Prince Faisal, through McLean, to do a thorough reconnaissance of the Royalist-held areas, and to write an appreciation of the situation giving recommendations as to what help the Royalists needed in men and supplies. Faisal seemed pleased with Smiley's report, and personally asked him to complete several more. He had suggested the use of European mercenaries as instructors in weapons and demolitions, mine laying, and as radio operators and medical orderlies.

The Royalist-Republican civil war carried on. Both sides made gains and losses in terms of territory. Initially, it had been thought that the 11,000 Egyptian troops would be able to advance from Hodeida to Sana in a matter of 14 days, and win (the Republicans in Cairo had told the CIA the same).[33] This never happened because of the terrible terrain (no paved roads) and Royalist opposition. Even though the Royalist army was outnumbered by Egyptian and Republican troops, the mercenary-trained Royalists (together with serving members of the SAS)[34] were, by 1967, able to hold 68,000 Egyptian troops in a stalemate situation.

Across in Saudi Arabia (Johnson and his team had moved their HQ from Aden) Johnson saw the Head of Saudi intelligence and explained: 'We can win – what do you want us to do? Go ahead or withdraw?' However, Saudi Arabia did not want the mercenary-backed Royalists to win because the Saudi government feared reprisal attacks by the Egyptian air force, which the Saudis could not match. Such attacks would have targeted main Saudi towns and cities; Jeddah had 'previously been overflown as a warning'.[35] The Egyptian Ambassador was in contact with the Saudi government and cautioned: 'You have moved to there, tut, tut, tut, if you move any further, we could retaliate.' So, according to Johnson, 'things never went too far, although we could have taken Sana'.

The British mercenary operation ended. This operation was significant in that it provided an avenue for the British government and SIS to fight against a coup, within which Philby had been involved, and the aftermath of it. But not all of the key members involved in the operation knew about Philby's assistance because it was handled on a 'need-to-know' basis.

Colonel Smiley did not know. 'I cannot ever remember his name being mentioned in this context. I would undoubtedly have remembered as in fact Philby was the direct cause of the failure of an operation that I was mounting into Albania when I was seconded from the army to MI6 [SIS] in 1949.'[36]

Colonel Johnson did not know. Colonel Stirling (who knew the SIS officer Nicholas Elliott) certainly knew,[37] although according to Colonel McLean 'Stirling didn't know that much [about Philby's involvement in the coup]'[38] but he knew enough. Obviously, McLean was not inhibited by the 'need-to-know' rule, because he did know; and this knowledge regarding Philby's involvement was a highly important factor in relation to the mercenary operation in response to the Philby-involved coup.

The coup in the Yemen was Philby's last job for the Soviet Union whilst in the Middle East. He had spent just over six years there, about which he is very reticent in his book *My Silent War*. In that text he states:

> [My] experiences in the Middle East from 1956 to 1963 do not lend themselves readily to narrative form except as part of the general history of the region during that period.[39]

However, Philby does give one or two hints about his Middle East role for the RIS – the obtaining of official documents:

> The fact is that the Soviet Union is interested in a very wide range of Middle East phenomena. Enjoying a wide margin of priority at the top of the list are the intentions of the United States and British governments in the area. For an assessment of such intentions, I was not too badly placed.[40]

He utilized informants:

> An hour's serious discussion with a trustworthy informant is often more valuable than any number of original documents. Of course, it is best to have both.[41]

Philby did not care to put questions to officials:

> If you put direct questions on matters of substance to any American or British official you are apt to get either an evasion or a whopping great lie.[42]

Not that he needed to, really. The British Ambassador in Cairo gave details to Nasser about SIS actions; and Nasser, who disliked the British, but knew how to make use of them, and had more time for the Americans, delighted in passing on to the Americans and the Russians the details of his talks.

Whilst in the Lebanon, Philby formed his own nucleus of contacts, both journalistic and intelligence. Here is a list of those contacts:

Tim Milne (SIS):	A friend from school days at Westminster School.
Mile Copeland (CIA):	Who watched Philby's travels with great interest.
Wilbur Crane Eveland (CIA):	A friend of Philby. They corresponded with each other.
Colonel Slade-Baker:	*Sunday Times* journalist and drinking companion.
Arthur Cooke:	Journalist and SIS employed. He and his wife lived in an apartment opposite to that of the Philbys' (in Beirut) and observed the same events.
Nicholas Elliott (SIS):	He set targets for Philby, sending him on trips, requested reports and shared some confidences.
Sam Brewer:	An American journalist. Eleanor, his wife, and Philby committed adultery. She subsequently became Philby's third wife.
(NAME CENSORED)	Journalist for the *Observer* Rumoured to be SIS-linked.
Professor Walid Khalidi:	At the American University in Beirut.
Willy Lazerus:	An Indian journalist in Cairo: was host to Philby in the capital.
Godfrey Janson:	A journalist in Beirut. Both he and Lazerus were anti-imperialist.
Glen Balfour-Paul:	The first Secretary at the British Embassy in Beirut.
Sir Pensonby Moore Crosthwaite:	The British Ambassador to Lebanon.
Peter Lunn (SIS):	He took over from Nicholas Elliott. Neither he nor Philby got on too well.
Harry Carr(SIS):	A long-time friend of Philby.
Ghosn Zogby (CIA):	Station Head in Beirut. He was introduced to Philby by Wilbur Crane Eveland.

Kermit Roosevelt (CIA):	In charge of CIA operations in the Middle East.
Kheiry Hammad:	Rumoured to be linked with SIS and Egyptian intelligence.
Sefton Delmer:	World War II 'black' propaganda officer and SIS linked.
Anthony Cavendish:	Former SIS officer.
Maurice Oldfield:	Security Service officer.
Dick Kallsen:	CBS employee.
Ralph Izzard:	*Daily Mail* journalist.
John Fistere:	King Hussein's CIA appointed public relations aide.
James Russell Barracks (CIA):	He masterminded CIA surveillance of Philby when in the Middle East.
Paul Paulson (SIS):	Station chief in Beirut. He had been at Westminster School with Philby and was later given the ask of keeping an eye on him to see if he was in touch with the RIS. He was also authorized to give Philby handouts for conducting minor intelligence activities. (Source: *Daily Telegraph*, 31 May 1987.)

Numerous Arab politicians, and the heads of Syrian, Egyptian, Turkish, Iraqi, Jordanian and Iranian intelligence organizations. Last but not least – George Blake.

In the early 1960s, Philby and Blake were together in Beirut, in close association with (and at) the Middle East College of Arabic Studies (MECAS); Blake had returned here in 1960. MECAS was located at Shemlar, near Beirut, and was often described as the British 'spy school'. It was financed and administered by the Foreign Office for training their officials as well as officials of the Consular and Colonial service, and also SIS and Military intelligence departments.

Philby and Blake were both in an ideal position to spot future SIS members. (They also talent-spotted for the RIS.) Indeed, when subsequently in Russia, Philby publicly blew the identity of the following SIS officers who had attended MECAS: Adrian Sindall, Peter Lunn, (also named by Blake as having initiated one of the most important telephone tapping operations whilst stationed in Germany) and Reginald Temple.

Whilst at MECAS, Blake sometimes received messages from SIS HQ summoning him to London[43] and although he was used to receiving such summonses, when in April 1961 he received one he became worried. Somehow he knew that SIS had uncovered him as an RIS agent. Blake feared that unless he returned to London he would be killed. As he subsequently explained to a close friend: 'They [SIS] could not let me be free. I bought my life by returning [otherwise I would have been killed] which gave me a chance to escape.' Blake had been 'fingered' by a Soviet defector called Golitsyn. Back in London, Blake found himself charged with spying for the Soviets, and was sentenced to an imprisonment of 42 years. Whilst in jail he became friendly with an aristocratic gentleman who described him: 'It was perfectly obvious that in all personal matters of family and finance, he was far from being a Communist. I have never met anyone less communistically inclined. However, he was the type of man who would sell secrets to anyone, and would gain a tremendous thrill in doing so. If he gave away the most crucial possible secrets for ten years it was not because he was a genuine Communist, but because he was a spy by nature. He got a kick from it, almost a sensual kick. He loved the feel of it.'[44]

Whilst in jail, Blake expected the RIS to 'spring' him. Despite feelers being made, the Soviets were not interested in arranging for his escape. Blake was pretty despondent. However, help was at hand. At one time, he was in the company of members of the CND who befriended him. Upon their release, they financed his escape by providing £700 to Sean Bourke, and his escape was duly arranged. But for the strong personality of one of Bourke's men, Blake would never have gone through with it. He had to be forced out of a window. Once Blake had escaped, CND members provided him with a nearby 'safe house' and a doctor in case of needs.

Information received by the author suggests that from 1964 to 1966 the prison authorities, the Home Office and the Security Service knew that Blake contemplated escape, hence the reason for the prison governor twice recommending his transfer. However, the Home Office refused to place him in secure conditions, and as we have seen, Blake escaped. He subsequently emerged in Moscow.

The aforementioned was written in 1986, and more or less covers the 'official' version. Since then the author has recently received new interesting information. When Blake returned from Beirut, SIS had a problem: they could not prove that Blake was an RIS agent nor produce any evidence which could be used in court. Blake, however, did not know that. SIS, therefore, offered him a 'deal' in return for a confession whereby Blake would receive a vastly reduced jail sentence. However, the Lord Chief Justice, Lord Parker, was not informed about any such 'deal', and instead sentenced Blake to 42 years – one year for each agent he had sent to his/her death. This was pure SIS disinformation somehow heard by Parker. Whilst in Germany Blake had been allowed by SIS to approach RIS as a so-called 'double' agent, and as part of his cover had been allowed to 'shop' SIS agents. Clearly, some of the deaths could be put at the door of SIS.[46]

Now SIS had another problem: it appeared that they had reneged upon their 'deal' with Blake, and the 42-year sentence could deter any future traitors from confessing. Blake had to be freed from jail. SIS men posing as CND activists* approached Bourke and the two CND Committee of 100 men, Michael Renolds and Pat Pottle, but they did not know that they were being used as 'front men' for the freeing of Blake. It is hard to believe that £700, allegedly provided by Blake's mother, would

---

* Committee of 100.

109

have covered the cost of the operation. It has been suggested that Tom Driburg, who worked for both the RIS and Security Service played a part in providing some of the cash.[47]

This all provides a fascinating story, especially when one takes into account how when interviewed by Phillip Knightley in Moscow, Philby suggested that SIS may have been involved in the springing of Blake.[48]

11

BACK IN THE USSR

Philby arrived back in the Soviet Union in early 1963. By now he was a habitual drunkard, if not an alcoholic; and found himself being 'dried out' in Kuibishev. He then was well and truly debriefed and provided all the information he could about SIS in the Middle East and elsewhere. This information was subsequently used by the RIS.

Philby was employed by the RIS as an officer and based in Moscow. Soon awards followed and he became a senior officer in the RIS hierarchy. In 1967 he was awarded the Order of the Red Banner, the second highest award in the USSR, and in 1970 he received their highest honour, the Order of Lenin.

In 1971 Philby was appointed head of the Department of Western Propaganda for the semi-official Novosti news agency. Novosti has been described as Russia's 'Bureau of Deception' and 'one of the most elaborate and expensive organs for deception in the entire Soviet propaganda machine' according to Western intelligence services. On 6 February 1980, the CIA tried to present a committee of the American House of Representatives with a rough breakdown of the enormous sums which the Soviet Union was spending on covert activity and propaganda. The grand total compiled from 16 operations was estimated at well over US $3 billion a year. Novosti was thought to account for US $500 million of this – accounting for the largest single item after Radio Moscow's foreign service and the Tass agency.

These agencies are always involved in disinformation campaigns when a Soviet citizen defects; coupled with this, the RIS makes an exhaustive 'damage report'. Once the report is completed, a copy is sent to the Department of Disinformation which in turn has received policy guidance directly from the Soviet Communist Central Committee for its campaign. A copy is also sent, say the experts, to the dreaded Department 13 of the first chief directorate, known colloquially in RIS terms as 'bloody affairs'. This department of the RIS is charged with retribution, enforcement and deterrent to other potential defectors through murder, assault or other violence. Sometimes, action is taken not only against a Soviet defector, but against anti-RIS moves made by the West. A case in point was in 1971 when the British government expelled 105 suspected Soviet agents from Britain. Philby counter-attacked by charging the expelling was to 'slow down the relaxation of tension in Europe'. Additionally, in an interview published in *Kodumaa* (13 October 1971, No. 41), he revealed details about his career with the 'British Intelligence Service' (BIS):

In the 1940s I had the opportunity to become well acquainted with the most protected and, therefore, the most dangerous operations of the BIS ...

The *Kodumaa* editor later queried:

We know that you worked for some time in the Near East, including Lebanon. We would like to hear about the British espionage undermining activities in that area, which through the fault of the imperialistic states has become the cause of tension during a number of years.

Philby replied:

112

Yes, I did work for quite a while in the Near East states. Even now I am interested in this area. The British Espionage and Intelligence Centre located in Beirut is active practically against all Arab states. After Peter Lunn, the leader of the English espionage there was WOMERSLEY, and currently it is DARBYSHIRE who works in the disguise of a secretary in the British Embassy. In the Embassy and in other English representative organisations the following have worked as agents:

McNAUGHT, RODERICK CLUBE (he was recently expelled from Baghdad because of espionage activities), RANDALL, CLIFFORD, WHITTAL, HOWARD, TEMPLE, ROWLEY, NOEL-CLARKE, STEEL, CHALMERS and others.

Presently such BIS representatives as WHITEBREAD, GOULTY, SPEDDING, are working there; people who have hidden themselves behind various diplomatic positions. Lebanon's British Embassy's First Secretaries SINDALL and JOY are also currently active on behalf of the British espionage system.

Reliable sources report that it was in Beirut that the SPA service group for the BIS was organised, that is the service who deals with falsification and provocations and if necessary with terror. The activity of the BIS residents in Arabia is first aimed at under-mining Arabian unity, compromising the leaders of the Arabian States who declare themselves in support of national unity and against imperialistic monopoly in the Near East. BIS agents, LIIBANONIS SOBHE BAKKARIT, MARUN ARABI, VAADIE MAALUFIT, were used during the late sixties to work against the Egyptian Embassy and to organise provocations against the Egyptian diplomats. For example, the English espionage organised the escape of JEHJA TAVIL, Arabian Delegation's First Secretary in Lebanon, to the West.

Beginning in 1959, BIS in Lebanon organised through its agents, several armed groups for acts of terror against unwanted activists in Lebanon. BIS established direct contact with the ultra rightist party leaders and in the early sixties prepared the overthrow of the lawful government of Lebanon and helped strengthen the military dictatorship.

Scores of names of Lebanon's citizen's whom BIS had engaged in espionage activities speak of the widespread activities of the English espionage system in Lebanon. Among these are Lebanon's counter-espionage(Suerte General) representatives A. R. BAYON, Lebanon's Parliamentary delegate ASPER ABMED, publisher and owner of a

Beirut newspaper R. ABELLA, Lebanon's Armed Services General Staff Worker MILAD KAREH. The British espionage system is also carrying out activities in other Arabian states. Special activities by the Great British espionage system are present in Amman where the BIS resident is British Embassy First Secretary SPEARES, and in Aden where the BIS resident is the British Embassy First Secretary BREHONY who exchanged the well known English spy K. HERDON.

The editor then asked:

Could you say a few words concerning the so-called psychological operations of BIS in the Near East?

Philby replied:

Such operations have poisoned the atmosphere of the Near East for decades and are organised by the BIS in practically all states. For example, the BIS resident prepared and distributed two anti-government brochures in Iraq in 1966. The BIS residency in Baghdad received much help from the BIS in Beirut where the skilled master of such operations PETER LUNN, with the help of BIS agent D. KUJAMDZAN, gave the final touch to the brochures and printed them on Arabian presses, procured through third parties, in the BIS headquarters.

BIS also used one of its other agents, former Iraq's oil chief ABDULLA ISHMAL, for undermining activities. Presently, BIS is activating a whole series of undermining activities in Egypt and Syria.

Using its position in Syrian emigration circles and the closeness of the former Syrian politician SALEEH DZEDDI, the BIS has during recent months alone published over fifteen 'Al-Samar'. The editorial staff of all these contains BIS paid agents who are active in the English espionage Near East 'psychological warfare' operations.

During the interview, Philby provided the barest of details of SIS operations in the Soviet Union. (Obviously, the Soviet Union did not want to admit to any SIS successes.) One major unpublished success occurred when Sir Stuart Menzies was the Chief of SIS. After Stalin's death, SIS considered that it was imperative to remove Beria, because they feared that if he rose to power, there might have been a Third World War. Therefore; SIS agents planted forged documents in the Kremlin incriminating him. The following day, after the documents had surfaced, Beria was taken out and shot.

Philby not only had details published in *Kodumaa* about SIS operations, but in *Izvestia* he charged that the following people in the Middle East were SIS agents and SIS officers:

Isbar, the elder son of a former Lebanese President, a Deputy in the Lebanese Parliament, and the man who formed the Ba'ath party.

Derry Shaver, First Secretary, Beirut.

Speares, First Secretary, Jordan.

Brehony, First Secretary, the Yemen (North) who had superseded Herdon 'a well-known British intelligence officer'.

Dori Chamoun, son of the former Lebanese President.

Emir Shekib Shehab, a former chief of Lebanese security.

Robert Abella, a journalist.

However, the allegations rebounded. In 1972 three of the above brought libel suits against TASS and were awarded damages: Shehab of £6,250; Abella, £6,250; and Isbar, £6,250.

Owing to the considerable amount of information Philby gained whilst in the Middle East, he was now in a position to assist RIS operations in Beirut. The Czechoslovak defector, and former security officer, Frantisek August testified that in the late 1960s the RIS were striving for total control of the Lebanon, and that in 1968 the RIS controlled in that country a network of 60 recruited agents ranging from a member of the Lebanese Communist Party's Politburo, through to agents in Kamal Jumblatt's party and other political parties. Members of the RIS, according to August, emphasized the great assistance they were receiving from Philby.[1]

Since that period the Soviets and Philby have constantly kept the Middle East in mind over the last few years.[2] Were the Soviets to have succeeded in bringing Lebanon into their orbit, they would have commanded an important position in the Mediterranean. Not that Soviet success is assured: both the Americans and the Israelis failed. Whether or not the Soviets should be successful, Philby was successful in terms of further awards. In 1980 he was awarded the Order of the Friendship of Peoples.[3]

As well as focusing on the Middle East, Philby and the Soviet Union also turned their attention to the nuclear arms and European peace movements. This interest over the past few years has partly been in response to the decision of certain Western governments[4] to deploy cruise and Pershing missiles on their soils. For some, in the case of West Germany, it was part of a deal with the Bonn government in the late 1970s whereby Germany agreed to stay within NATO provided that the missiles were introduced in Europe.

The idea that the Soviet Union has directly or even indirectly been involved inside European peace movements has been hotly and totally denied by left-wing groups. However, the Soviets have indeed made their involvement clear.

> The Communists' line in the peace movements is absolutely clear. Even their enemies acknowledge that no other political organisation has done as much to strengthen the peace movements as have the Communists.
> Professor Mikhail Bazmanov, 'Communists and pacifists in the 1980s', *Soviet Weekly*, 19 February 1983

> In the Soviet Union there is a massive and democratically organised peace movement with the affiliation of trade unions, women's and youth's organisations millions strong.
> *The New Worker*, 18 February 1983

> Anti-war actions and events are organised by trade unions, by youth and woman's organisations, by professional bodies, by scientific societies and the Church. Their actions are united by the Soviet Peace Committee which belongs to the World Peace Council[5] and which, among other things, co-ordinates the actions of the Soviet public with the world-wide peace movement.
> Alexander Smirnov, 'The anti-war movements in the USSR'.
> *Soviet Weekly*, 5 February 1983

The peace movements in the Socialist [Communist movement] does not avoid these meetings [with peace movements in the West]. On the contrary, it encourages them and seeks a dialogue with the peace movements in the West. For years, it has been cooperating with national peace organisations associated with the World Peace Council, and it has also established contacts with other peace organisations and movements.

Vladimir Novak, 'For peace and life, against Nuclear war'.
The New Worker, 28 January 1983

The September 1983 issue of the Soviet ideological journal, *Communist*, laid bare with startling candour Moscow's tactics for taking control of the international peace movement. The journal's leading articles spelt out about the Communists already working within the Western trade unions, anti-nuclear groups, pacifist organizations and even environmental groups, who are opposed to the United States and its NATO Allies. It said that some Western Communists had been too slow in infiltrating such groups, now this was being corrected. The Communist parties of West Germany, France, Greece, Austria, Sweden, Switzerland and the United States all got a pat on the back for their efforts along these lines. But the journal said that some Western Communists were slow to exploit independent pressure groups, although it adds that these defects are being overcome; it also states that Communists should consider active participation in such organizations who had a crucial means of consolidating ties with the public and strengthening their influence on the organizations concerned. 'Communists are stepping up their activities in factories and trade unions,' the article added.

According to a former SOE officer (later SIS-linked), with regard to the strategy of the Soviet Union and the peace movements in the West, Philby 'looks things over and gives his advice'. We shall analyse what has been achieved, thanks in part to Philby-masterminding, country-by-country.

117

International Information
Department (IID)

├─

International Department (ID)
of CPSU Central Committee,
Moscow

├─

Responsible for CPSU relations
with:
– Non-ruling Communist
  parties
– Revolutionary democratic
  parties
– Left Socialists
– National liberation
  movements
– International fronts
– Friendship societies

Committee for State Security
(KGB) (included General
Philby):

Service A – active measures,
disinformation.

├─

World Peace Council, Helsinki
(135 affiliates)

Publishes *New Perspective
Peace Courier*.
Permanent representatives at
UN, New York and Geneva,
UNESCO, Paris.

International Committee for
  European Security and
  Co-operation, Brussels.
International Campaign
  Committee for a Just Peace
  in The Middle East.
International Committee of
  Solidarity with the Arab
  People and their Central
  Cause – Palestine, Tripoli.
International Committee on
  Southern Africa.
Movement for the Peace and
  Sovereignty of the Peoples,
  Havana.

118

Soviet Committee for Defence of Peace, Moscow Soviet Peace Fund	Novosti Press Agency: Philby's Department of Western Propaganda.

Tass;
Izvestia;
Aeroflot;
Soviet Life (Published in
  Washington, DC)
New Times;
World Marxist Review: Sponsors
  Problems of Peace and
  Democratic Organizations
  Commission.

India	Panama
Cuba	Lebanon
Vietnam	Bulgaria
Syria	Iraq
Australia	Italy
Poland	Argentina
Guinea	Soviet Union
France	United States
Ethiopia	E. Germany
Portugal	Finland
Palestine	Jordan
UK	Hungary
Angola	Czechoslovakia
Egypt	Chile
Zimbabwe	Madagascar
African National Congress	Mali

This chart denotes how Philby had a pivotal position both in Novosti as Head of the Department of Western Propaganda, and in the RIS.

Norway

Among the citizens of Norway, neutralist tendencies are somewhat strong. Indigenous peace movements tend not to be particularly dominated by the Communists. In Norway the local Communist parties are relatively weak and isolated. However, the Soviets have made gains within the Parliament of Norway. In late 1983, Arne Treholt, a senior Norwegian foreign ministry official, was arrested and charged with spying for the USSR. Whilst a state official, he supported the idea of a Scandinavian nuclear-free zone, and propagated the idea to Jens Everson (for whom he worked as Personal Secretary in 1973–76 and as his Deputy Minister in 1976–79). It was a speech by Everson in October 1980, which converted the Norwegian Labour Party to support the introduction of a nuclear-free zone. Both Treholt and Everson opposed EEC membership. (Treholt was adviser to Everson when he was negotiating an agreement with the EEC after Norway's rejection of EEC membership.) Everson is not suspected of involvement in Treholt's espionage. Security sources believe that Treholt's case may have been controlled in Oslo by a Third Secretary at the Soviet Embassy, Stanislav Schebotok, who has been identified as an RIS officer. His speciality was asserted to be the infiltration of political circles, and through them, of Norwegian peace movements (NPM). *Neve Zurcher Zeitung* of 26 November 1981, reported that Schebotok was under suspicion of having 'doubtful contacts' with members of the NPM and had personally addressed their gatherings. Direct Soviet funding had also occurred. On 4 June 1981, Norway's Art for Peace group held a meeting at the Peoples' House in Oslo. This meeting had been funded by the Soviet Embassy. Also in June 1981, it became known that 'Art for Peace' had received other funds from the Soviet Lada car factory. On 28 November 1981, following these revelations, two Soviet diplomats were expelled from Norway for masterminding such activities.

Denmark

On 21 October 1981, the visa of Vladimir Merkulov, Second Secretary at the Soviet Embassy in Copenhagen, was suddenly cancelled. (Merkulov had succeeded Schebotok when the latter had been accused by the Danish press of clandestine contacts with persons suspected of having been recruited as Soviet agents.) As Second Secretary, Merkulov had fed Soviet funds into the Danish 'Co-operation for Peace and Security' (CCPC) – an umbrella organization for no fewer than 59 different peace groups – which was used to finance advertisements in Danish newspapers favouring the idea of a nuclear-free zone in Northern Europe. The CCPC was both founded and inspired by the World Peace Council (WPC)[5] in 1973 following a WPC meeting in Moscow attended by 31 Danes. This beginning was explained by CCPC Secretary, Carl Rosschou. CCPC member, Arne Herlov Peterson, received money from RIS officer Merkulov. It is now known that for two years, the Danish Police Counter-Espionage Service (PET) had been watching the same Danish journalist, Arne Herlov Peterson, who with his wife, was arrested and charged with espionage on 4 November 1981. Over the preceding eighteen months, Merkulov had 23 secret meetings with him. One of their joint projects was the financing of an appeal in favour of a 'Nuclear-free Scandinavian Zone' to which 150 Danish artists naïvely lent their names. PET officers were reported by the *Beringske Tidende* (8 November 1981) to have admitted that 'there were so many KGB officers in Denmark that it was impossible with its present framework to keep a watch on all of them'. When they did raid the Peterson's home, diaries recording the financial transactions and books containing over 3,000 names were seized. After these dis-closures, prominent members of the Danish Social Democratic Party (SDP) publicly appealed to 'the more serious part of the peace movement' not to identify itself with groups that could have been infiltrated by the RIS. Additionally, the Social Democratic newspaper, *Aktuett*, on 6 November 1981, noted that 'hundreds of Danish peace-advocating artists find themselves in the situation that they have been pawns in an international manoeuvre'.

Three years later, Lev Mendelevich was posted to Denmark to become the Soviet Ambassador, along with RIS officer Nikolai Shatskh. Western security services noted that the two Soviets were officials of a higher standing than usual, and feared that Kremlin leaders saw Denmark as a country which could be drawn out of NATO and into neutrality.

West Germany

In West Germany, the Federal (Social Democratic) Government in Bonn, on 20 January 1982, replied officially to a relevant parliamentary question from a group of CDU-CSU MPs.

> There is evidence that DKP [German Communist Party] has been receiving considerable [financial] contributions from the German Democratic Republic [East Germany]. This has been pointed out repeatedly by the Federal Government. The orthodox Communist campaign against the NATO dual-track decision [i.e. for NATO's nuclear modernization programme) is part of the Party's activities in the DKP. The security authorities do not dispose of further findings.

According to a secret investigation by Bundesnachrichtendienst (West Germany's equivalent of the CIA) the Soviet Union had surreptitiously been pumping US $30 million annually into the West German peace movement, including the Green Party, which in 1983, held 27 seats in Parliament. The funds were channelled into the country through front organizations.

Moreover, in the same context, it is well worth recalling that a former member of the East German Communist Party's Central Committee's 'West' section, Fritz Teppich, then the West Berlin correspondent of the East German News Agency, played a major role in arranging the much-publicized Bonn Anti-Nuclear demonstration of *circa* 300,000 on 10 October 1981.

122

Switzerland

During April 1983, the Swiss government accused the Soviet Union of behind-the-scenes involvement in the Swiss anti-nuclear power movement. The Geneva police had discovered anti-nuclear power tracts among baggage from a Russian Aeroflot airliner. The tracts were directed against a Swiss nuclear power project at Keisersaugst, near Basle. In consequence, the Berne bureau of the Russian news agency, Novosti, was closed because the Swiss authorities said that it was operating as a 'centre for subversion'. The bureau's director, Alexi Dumov, was given until 8 May to leave the country. In an unusually stern and explicit note handed to the Russian Embassy in Berne, the Swiss government said that it would 'act resolutely and with all means' to resist Russian interference in its domestic affairs. A government statement said that the Berne bureau of Novosti had 'served as a centre for disinformation, subversion and agitation' rather than as a news agency. 'Activities at Novosti in Berne did not involve espionage, but efforts to subvert public opinion in Switzerland' a spokesman for the Swiss Ministry of Justice said.

The Swiss government statement alleged that the news bureau had been used as a centre for the 'political and ideological indoctrination' of young members of the Swiss peace anti-nuclear and conscientious objectors' movements and for planning street demonstrations.

Holland

On 6 and 13 November 1982, the Amsterdam daily, *De Telegraaf*, reported an analysis by Netherland's security of Soviet and East European efforts to influence the Dutch peace movement. The 6 November article, spoke of 'clear proof of Soviet involvement' and of close co-operation between the Dutch Communist Party and the International Department of the Soviet Communist Party in the campaign against NATO's nuclear weapons. The 13 November article stated: 'The Soviet authorities are still actively influencing the Netherlands debate on NATO nuclear weapons modernisation.' *De Telegraaf* further stated that a key individual in the Soviet effort was Anatoli Povov, who headed a Soviet delegation to Holland for talks on the peace movement in January 1982, and was an official of the International Department of the Soviet Communist Party.

Vadim Leonov, a Tass correspondent, found himself leaving Holland after losing his accreditation as a Soviet journalist. He had been caught by Dutch security when he tried to bribe a Dutch Defence Ministry officer into revealing state secrets. Additionally, he had the mission of passing on not only information, but sometimes orders, to groups within the Dutch peace movement (which contains a strong left-wing orientation and includes Communist-front organizations). In one remarkably unguarded moment, Leonov boasted to a Dutch journalist friend that he (Leonov) could line up a demonstration of 50,000 easily in Holland – one message via his channels would suffice. He further described his daily job as being able to pass on messages from Moscow to peace groups in Europe.

The peace movements and organizations in Holland had been of much interest to the Soviet Union, because these organizations have been in the vanguard of campaigns to block the development of the neutron warhead and the plan to install cruise missiles. One such organization was a committee called 'Stop the neutron bomb – stop the nuclear arms race', which include several leaders of the Dutch Communist Party. One other committee called 'Christians for Socialism' was viewed as being a Communist front, and according to security sources, at least one of their Dutch members had been trained in East Germany. The 'No to Cruise Committee' was an extremely potent force.

Overall, the Soviets and Philby, had no reason to complain about Holland. After all, the Dutch parliament nearly decided not to deploy 48 new US nuclear weapons in Holland. Instead the government agreed not to deploy cruise missiles by 1986, as originally planned (by NATO), but by the end of 1988, and then only if the Soviets continued to expand their number of

SS-20s. Prime Minister Rudd Lubbers added that Holland would cut back on the 48 missiles it had agreed to deploy if the United States and the Soviet Union could reach an agreement to limit the number of intermediate-range missiles before November 1985.

Further confirmation about the role of the Soviet Union and the peace movements in Europe came in 1997 with the publication of the autobiography of the former chief of the East German Foreign Intelligence Service, Markus Wolf. He confirms how the movements received financial support from the Soviet bloc, and also adds:

> My role as head of foreign intelligence, with a good knowledge of the political climate in Western Europe, was to concentrate on the efforts of the disarmament campaign on the foreign policies of the NATO countries and to work out how the East could profit from divisions within the Western alliance on this emotional issue.

As we have seen, his work and that of Philby were very effective indeed. Wolf and Philby met several times in East Germany. Philby recounted how SIS in Moscow found ways of making several offers for him to return to the West. One wonders if he mentioned to Wolf about his bouts of depression, alcoholism and attempted suicides; he also complained bitterly to Wolf about the miserable economy and the gap between the rulers and the people. Wolf took the view that Philby was lucky and died in time (1988) before the collapse of (what the Soviets perceived to be) Communism.

12

THE PHILBY JIGSAW

Following his exposure as a Soviet agent, Philby's psyche became the object of wholesale comment and analysis, unique in the history of espionage. As Philby recorded in his book *My Silent War*, 'Explanations of extraordinary silliness were offered in preference to the obvious truth'. The simple truth was that during his Cambridge days he had become a Communist. 'It was a slow and brainracking process; my transition from a Socialist viewpoint to a Communist one took two years. It was not until my last term at Cambridge, in the summer of 1933, that I threw off my last doubts. I left university with a degree and with the conviction that my life must be devoted to Communism.' Philby's statement somewhat obfuscates the matters. When he says that only during his last term did he throw off his last doubts, one is given the impression that he only became a Communist in the summer of 1933. Further, by adding that he left university 'with the conviction' that his life be devoted to Communism, he gives the impression that he had not been recruited to become a Soviet agent until leaving university.

Philby's progression to Communism had been observed by his friend Tim Milne. They had been together at Westminster School, and both had subsequently joined SIS. After leaving school, Milne went up to Christ Church, Oxford, and Philby to

Trinity, Cambridge. During weekends they met at Philby's home and maintained their friendship. At Christ Church, Milne talked a great deal about him; he hero-worshipped Kim. During college vacations they travelled together. In 1932 they travelled to Germany (Berlin), Hungary and Austria, to see what was happening. Professor Hugh Trevor-Roper, who lived on the same staircase as Milne at Christ Church, recalls Milne talking of his 'Communist' travelling companion, Kim Philby. Clearly, Philby was a Communist before 1933.

The most reasonable explanation one can give for his obfuscations in *My Secret War*, first published in 1968, is that he did not want the University of Cambridge, and in particular Trinity College, noted as a recruiting ground for the Soviets. After all, the security services had only to look at Trinity in the early 1930s and the Philby-Burgess circle in order to discover more of the Soviet-recruited agents, including Michael Straight and Anthony Blunt, and especially look at the Apostles society, which was a centre of both homosexuality and Communism.

During his first two years at Trinity Philby remained inconspicuous, and involved himself, even voiced moderate sentiments, in the Labour Club: and during the 1931 elections he canvassed for the Labour candidate of the Cambridge constituency. His close friends, such as Whitney Straight, later chief executive of BOAC, and deputy chairman of Rolls-Royce, and Victor Rothschild, later a brilliant biochemist, and Security Service officer, could not be suspected of an inclination towards Communism.

Also at Trinity – he had arrived in 1930 – was Guy Francis Money Burgess, an old Etonian and son of a distinguished Royal Navy officer. Burgess, the Pied Piper of Trinity, radiating unlimited energy, and drawing people to him like a magnet, soon had his own circle. Within it was young Kim Philby. Other remarkable undergraduates also joined it, including James Klugman, who became a leading member of the British Communist Party (CP), and, as we shall see, a recruiting agent for the

RIS; John Cornford, a history research student; David Haden-Guest, son of a Labour peer; Anthony Blunt who was recruited by the RIS; Francis Edward Cumming-Bruce, son of Lord Thurlow, and later a distinguished diplomat and knight.

It would be wrong to assume that all of the Philby-Burgess circle became pro-Soviet or RIS agents. Indeed, some of the brilliant undergraduates later became stalwart Conservatives; only Burgess, Cornford and Klugman declared themselves Communists at Cambridge; others had a socialism of various degrees from pale to shocking pink.

It has often been assumed that the members, and aquaintances, of the Philby-Burgess-the-Apostles circles mainly became British security or intelligence officers. Many did, others did not; Richard Clarke, known to nurse radical sympathies (he once argued 'that a revolution of some kind was necessary') became a diplomat; Brian Simon became a member of the Central Committee of the British CP; Hume Boggis-Rolfe, rose to a high position in the Lord Chancellor's office (his brother Paul joined SIS); and Carl Aavold had a distinguished legal career as did Steven Chapman.

Whilst at Trinity Philby met 'the Lord' (for legal reasons he cannot be named) who is alleged to have 'talent-spotted' Philby, Blunt, Burgess and others who cannot be named.

The Western governments all know who he is and what he has done. None has ever dared to name him still less remove him. In fact, it would be very difficult to work out a legal case. After all, is it possible to prosecute a man who has never taken out a single document from the files of any department and who has never written one single illegal word?

Born into a family of immense wealth at the close of the Edwardian era 'the Lord' was heir to a place in the highest inner society. He has occupied positions in the two most secret and sensitive official offices; he selected for one office some of the most dangerous of the known, and unknown, Soviet agents.

As one knowledgeable source has written: 'Government after

government has been too scared to touch him and indeed no Attorney General has been able to advise a prosecution, because not one scrap of paper exists. What is known consists of a complicated tissue of extremely clever devices, none of which can be proved in a Court of Law as treachery, still less a violation of the Official Secrets Act'.[1]

Here is an example of 'the Lord's' influence. He advised Churchill in 1942 that the Russians felt that Kenneth de Courcy (who we shall meet later in this chapter), who was highly critical towards Russia,[2] should be locked up under Section 18b. Moscow asserted that de Courcy's influence was postponing the opening of a Second Front. In fact, such an opinion was ridiculous. But such was Stalin's belief. 'The Lord' was ordered to see Churchill about it. He three times pressed Churchill who none the less refused.[3]

However, 'the Lord' was a man of ruthless determination, and it is believed he made up his mind to obtain revenge. It so happened some sixteen years later that de Courcy was anxious to sell a large estate (or part of it) to finance anti-Communist activities. Four hundred houses on the estate were applied for by the public and four hundred proper legal contracts were duly executed. Each purchaser (without exception) required a mortgage. Owing, it is believed, to the activities of 'the Lord's' financial office in the city institutions, not one applicant for a mortgage was accepted and the entire four hundred house purchases failed to complete.

'The Lord' then organized some of his most important contacts (including a former SIS officer, who had been at Trinity College with Blunt and co.) to issue a false prospectus on the London market (it was issued). By extremely clever moves de Courcy was introduced to buy shares costing some £400,000. As soon as that was done 'the Lord' collapsed the market. The shares fell and dealings were suspended.

Because 'the Lord' had a powerful man in a Legal Department, and men in the judiciary (all the men were at Trinity with Blunt and co.) and in the police, no one was prosecuted.[4]

129

Whilst at Cambridge Philby and co. mixed with people who subsequently became very famous indeed. One such person, as mentioned, was Victor Rothschild. As a young man, Rothschild was at Trinity College at the same time as Burgess and Blunt. Unlike the other Rothschilds in Europe, Victor was to the left, and it is believed looked for like-minded companions to 'recruit' and enter a small left-wing circle. He met Guy Burgess and they developed a deep and lasting friendship. On occasions Burgess visited the Rothschild family seat in the country. During one visit Burgess met Rothschild's mother who – prior to the meeting – was vastly impressed by what her son had told her about his friend's political insight. During the meeting, Mrs Rothschild listened to a summing up of world affairs by Burgess who opined as to how these affairs, in various parts of the world, affected the Rothschild empire. She was so impressed that she decided to engage the services of Burgess, dispose with the financial brains and advice within the Rothschild empire, and pay Burgess a retainer of £100 per month (a very healthy sum in those days) in return for advice on her personal investments.

'That at least is the story which has gone down for the record, but it is one for which the imagination boggles. The picture of a young man supplanting the highly qualified financial advisors to one of the richest women in the world can only be accepted by the most gullible.'[5] But other less gullible observers have assigned a more believable verdict: recruitment into work of a minor role for one of the Jewish intelligence groups. At that time anti-Semitism was on the upsurge, and was rampant in Germany. Therefore, leading Jews – including the Rothschilds – were very concerned indeed. Because Burgess was due to travel abroad in Europe quite often, he was to be in a useful position as an observer. It was shortly after this that he made the first of many trips to Germany.

In addition to travelling into Europe, Burgess ingratiated himself with right-wing pro-German/Nazi elements in Britain.

He became Secretary and Personal Assistant, occasional travelling companion, and friend to Captain Jack Macnamara, a right-wing MP for Chelmsford who had close ties with the Nazis. In candid moments 'Guy would joke about the homosexual encounters he had taken part in with Macnamara and his Nazi friends. In a moment of elated intoxication, he would hint that he had learned something of importance through the indiscretion of a Nazi diplomat'.[6] Macnamara was an important member of the Anglo-German Fellowship, a pro-German body. Burgess became a member, which provided him with many useful right-wing acquaintances and contacts. His most important contact was Edouard Pfeiffer, a homosexual, petty radical, and Cabinet Chief to the French Prime Minister, Daladier.[7]

When Burgess returned from abroad he lived in Rothschild's London flat at 5 Bentinck Street which was 'leased for the duration by Victor Rothschild to Burgess'.[8] Maclean was an occasional visitor to the flat where Burgess stayed with Blunt,[9] who was in permanent residence there.[10] Philby was also a visitor; together with Rothschild, but not so often as from 1940 when security service work took Rothschild away. Both Blunt and Rothschild were employed by the Security Service. Indeed, Rothschild recruited Blunt into the service and was aware of Blunt's Marxist convictions: 'and it would be naïve to presume that he was planting a potential Russian spy in Britain's most exclusive security service ... Anthony Blunt was not selected in spite of his Marxist sympathies. They were in fact his passport to preferment.'[11]

Just as Rothschild had met and befriended Burgess at Cambridge, the same applied to Blunt. Rothschild had met Blunt in 1931 when he was 21 years old and Blunt was 24. They discussed politics. Coming from an upper-middle-class background, Blunt was fascinated by the Rothschild wealth, power and prestige. Rothschild slightly opened a most seductive door to areas Blunt had never seen before, and Blunt was captivated. He also was not rich. After all, Rothschild had to provide him with £100 in

1932 to buy Poussin's 'Rebecca at the well'. Blunt was very grateful indeed; and, it is believed, joined what was a small left-wing pro-Soviet group within which Rothschild, according to one expert, was 'the most influential'. Burgess was also in the group. He and Rothschild subsequently recruited Blunt into the Apostles society 'a [partly homosexual] recruiting ground for Soviet Secret Service agents',[12] from which Michael Straight, Blunt, Burgess and others were recruited. All were pro-Soviet. That Rothschild was pro-Soviet was observed by Malcolm Muggeridge at a meeting in Paris at the Rothschilds' mansion in the Avenue Marigny; Philby was also present. There was a heated discussion at their dining table 'about the rights and wrongs of withholding important Bletchley intercepts from the Soviet Union'.[13] The matter was raised by Rothschild who startled Muggeridge 'by the vehemence in criticising [the] standard practice of withholding certain information from the Russians, because, as Rothschild argued, such information "would be invaluable to the Russians... To deny such vital information was worse than an unfriendly act".'[14] Philby violently agreed, in such a manner that Muggeridge suspected treachery on Philby's behalf. (One can only guess as to his thoughts about Rothschild.) After the end of the war, Rothschild, it is believed, left behind his left-wing views, and pro-Soviet attitude, to become established and one of the establishment. He became a scientist, banker and administrator, and then a Lord.

Rothschild's role was, and still is, most interesting in terms of his circle of Cambridge friends and aquaintances, 'talent spotting' and 'recruitment'. There is little wonder when his friends pointed out that publishing that he recruited Blunt into the Security Service would have embarrassed him.[15]

It has been assumed by many observers that because of his association with four of the major Soviet agents, Rothschild was the so-called fifth man. He was not. As we shall discover, he was the first man.

*   *   *

Upon graduating from Cambridge, Philby went to Vienna, and, as an RIS agent, came under the control of Walter Krivitsky, the chief of Soviet military intelligence in Western Europe, who directed agents in Germany, Holland, Switzerland, Italy and Austria up until 1937.[16] As one of Krivitsky's agents, Philby served as a courier for Krivitsky's network in Hungary. Whilst in Vienna, Philby married a young Jewish girl, Litzi Friedman, with whom he returned to England. She was also a Communist. From then on, Philby's career was guided by the RIS: his shift of politics to become a pro-Nazi sympathizer and his assignment as a journalist on Franco's side of the Spanish Civil War must have been their invention. It was during his assignment with the British forces in Europe that he was instructed, according to Philby, to direct his efforts towards securing a position in one of the British security or intelligence services. As we saw in chapter 1, he succeeded within a year.

By this time, Britain and Russia were at war with Germany. But one of the Soviet Union's fears was that Britain and Germany would conclude a separate peace agreement, thus leaving Germany to defeat the USSR. Meanwhile, across in Germany, Rudolf Hess had become alarmed about the war and the Nazi excesses. He believed that a total reversal of strategy and policy was essential. He had heard stories that Queen Mary, the Duke of Windsor, the Dukes of Westminster and Buccleuch, the Marquis of Londonderry, Lords Halifax and Rushcliffe, Basil Liddell Hart and R. A. Butler thought so too. His idea was the evacuation of France, Belgium, Norway and Denmark, peace with England and the placement of Jews in Palestine. He knew that the former President, Herbert Hoover, Ambassador Hugh Gibson, Charles Lindbergh and many others in America, thought the same, as did, of course, Pétain, Laval and Mussolini. War with the Soviet Union would, however, be continued.

With his plan and peace proposals, Hess flew to Britain and landed in Scotland at the Duke of Hamilton's estate. As Hitler's

133

deputy leader, and his most fanatical supporter, he was in a very important position and was not to be ignored. Hess was taken into general custody, to the Tower of London, and on to a private house near Windsor where he remained to the end of the war. There he was guarded by army officers, within the military district of Colonel Pilcher. Both the German and British governments let it be known that Hess was 'half-mad' or 'insane', after all, he was an embarrassment to both governments. Had Prime Minister Churchill shown any interest in Hess's proposals, he would have found himself violently attacked by pro-Soviet elements. The Russians knew that Hess was planning Russia's destruction and was ready to concede to the Western powers. That was unforgivable in Russian eyes. Hence, Hess was branded as being 'insane' – yet he was not insane enough not to appear before the Nuremberg War Trials in 1945 when the Soviets charged that he was the greatest war criminal of them all. His sanity was observed by Colonel Pilcher, who told an observer on 28 May 1941:

We know that Hess is not suffering from any serious illness or insanity. Our observer in Stockholm reports that a close Swedish friend of Hess who visited him in Munich several times recently saw no signs of illness of any sort. Why did this man Hess, who held a position of immense importance, leave the trappings of power for a hazardous flight into the heart of the enemy territory? If he came with a mission entrusted to him by powerful forces in Germany, then more than he alone must feel exactly the same. Germany has problems and they must be pressing ones. In all probability they centre around the political dangers inherent in a long war. The one man in Europe who certainly knows the innermost details of the whole business is Admiral Canaris [head of the Abwehr]. There is nothing which happens in Germany of which the Admiral does not know.

The recipient of the above information suggests that there was little, if anything, known to Canaris which was not also known to Major General Sir Stewart Menzies, then the Chief of SIS, and that both officers (Canaris and Menzies) frequently met in Spain, and that Canaris was determined that Hitler should not, repeat not, defeat Britain. Should Hess have arrived in Britain knowing about Canaris – and his real aim was to topple Hitler before a total world war developed then it was of crucial importance to pro-Soviet elements, including Philby and his circle, to stop Hess. Churchill knew that Pilcher was officially aware of Hess's own story. He also knew that Pilcher and Menzies were very close friends and of the connection between Canaris and Menzies. However, Pilcher threatened to leak the facts. At that time he was commanding the Grenadier Guards at Windsor. He was, therefore, dealt with by being relieved of his command and compelled to go into hospital for an operation (to cover his sudden evaporation). Thereafter he was ordered to Scotland. He lived the rest of his life under virtual house arrest until he died in 1970. In 1941, the seventh Marquis of Londonderry saw the then Secretary of State for War to ask for an explanation of Colonel Pilcher's fate. All comment was refused. Similarly, a (now) titled man approached Menzies. Menzies replied that all enquiries were viewed with extreme disfavour. The secret papers of the Hess case have been disclosed, but not exposed and released to the general public. Pilcher's name disappeared from *Who's Who?* When an explanation was sought, none was forthcoming – except that his address had been mislaid. Years later Pilcher's close friend, Marshal of the Royal Air Force Lord Newall was asked. He replied: 'No comment'.

The Hess case has been written about in detail. Moreover, the case highlights the situation where the Soviet Union did not want a separate peace to arise between Germany and the West, as this would have led to Russian defeat. Philby certainly concurred. As head of the Iberian Section, and later head of Section IV, he was in a position to hear of any peace feelers from Germany and act accordingly. For example, when he was head of the Anti-Soviet Section (IV), he was in charge of reading the Abwehr code, and was able to discern the true and fake peace-makers. His Russian masters were obviously anxious to prevent any peace overtures from elements inside Germany, made through the Allies, especially one which attached armistice conditions concerning the penetration of Germany by the Red Army. Philby, therefore made a point of intercepting and destroying the communications from dissident Germans. Towards the end of the war, Canaris plotted to overthrow Hitler; he was caught out in the plot, and subsequently executed (hanged – it took eight attempts) for treason. The information which led to his arrest came from the USSR. Moscow had received the tip-off from Philby, who it would appear caused World War II to be extended.

It did not matter at all how many people Philby directly, or at arm's length, caused to be captured, imprisoned or shot. At the beginning of this book we saw how he caused the death of the would-be Soviet defector, Volkov. He even caused 'problems' for officers and agents who worked for both Britain and Russia. A case in point is that of the dedicated RIS operative, Alexander Rado, who headed the Lucy Ring. It is possible that without the incredibly detailed information sent to the Soviet Union from Rado, the Russians would have lost the war. He was censured by Moscow, among his other 'crimes', for passing information to Britain about Hitler's V2 rockets. Such information was of no value to the Soviet Union because of the short range of the V2. However, Moscow disapproved of giving Britain any assistance that would help lessen the bombardment of London. Following the closure of the Lucy Ring by the Swiss authorities, after protests from Germany, Rado went to the Russian Embassy in Paris seeking work. From there he was flown to Cairo en route for Moscow. In Cairo, he toyed with the idea of defecting to Britain, and was seen by the SIS officer, Maurice Oldfield, who contacted SIS HQ London for guidance. The telegram was handled by Philby, who after consulting his Soviet controller, instructed Oldfield to ensure that Rado went on to Moscow. After arriving in Moscow he was awarded 10 years' imprisonment for his heroic work for the Soviet Union.

During his two years as head of Section IX, Philby monitored not only the efforts against Russia, but also the identity and personality of British officers and agents, a close-up view of its file system and office procedure, its budget and tables of organization. He also maintained close contact with his opposite number, the Security Service officer, Roger Hollis, an alleged Soviet agent. Additionally, Philby's place on the Joint Intelligence Subcommittee on Communist affairs widened his knowledge, and all the information was duly passed onto his Russian controller.

His total access to classified information went even further than intelligence matters. He had access to hundreds of classified documents from the Foreign Office, the War Office, the Admiralty, and the Cabinet Secretariat. His total worth to the RIS was virtually incalculable. The Soviets certainly did not want to lose Philby, who for years had been very lucky not being 'blown'. However, certain people were beginning to show an interest in him. One such person was the CIA officer, James Jesus Angleton. Both had met during World War II when they worked together. Angleton's suspicion was first raised at the end of 1945, when he heard Philby remark unexpectedly, after receiving the Order of the British Empire (OBE) at Buckingham Palace from King George VI, that 'This country could do with a stiff dose of proper Socialism'. At the time Philby made his utterance, both the National Security Agency in America, in an operation code-named U-TRAFFIC, and the code-breaking organization at Eastcote in England, were involved in reading codes. The volume of traffic going to Moscow from the Soviet Consulate in New York had been noticeably heavier during the summer of 1945. The code-breakers eventually discovered that the Russians appeared to have their own source inside the British Embassy in Washington who bore the code-name HOMER, and who had sent the details of secret telegrams between Attlee and President Truman to the Russians. But the identity of the British official was not known.

Philby, as we have seen in chapter 4, arrived in Washington in

1949. He made the mistake however, of associating with Burgess and Maclean. By September 1949, Angleton received powerful information from an Israeli source about Philby. Teddy Kollek, now the Mayor of Jerusalem, visited Washington on official business, and in a corridor of the CIA HQ saw Philby at a distance. He then told his CIA acquaintances that in 1934 he had witnessed Philby marrying a member of the Communist underground. He added: 'once a Communist, perhaps always a Communist.' Now Angleton's suspicions were totally aroused, and following the unsuccessful operations in Albania he was quite sure that Philby was a Soviet agent.

In 1951 a lucky slip, or a specially placed item of information for the eyes-only of Maclean, in U-TRAFFIC identified him as being a Soviet agent. Clyde (later General) Rich, US Air Force, found that Maclean had a top security clearance in Washington and was going through files at night. Rich tried to have Maclean's security lifted. Instead of denying Maclean access to the files, American security saw to it that Rich was transferred. Rich also discovered that Burgess and Maclean wanted to visit an ultra-secret project in Los Alamos, New Mexico. At that time Rich was deputy to General Ian Anderson, then head of Plans and Operations in the Pentagon. He and Rich agreed that no foreigner, even the British, should have access to such a secret project, and it was for this reason a directive was issued by Anderson that Burgess and Maclean were forbidden permission. 'Later,' according to Rich,[17] 'we realized how right we were.'

U-TRAFFIC material provided further information to be used against Philby. Bill Harvey, from the FBI's Office of Security, wrote a comprehensive report for his FBI chief, J. Edgar Hoover, on what he saw as Philby's duplicity. During this time, Philby had received a secret report stating that Maclean was HOMER, and in Philby's words:

It was essential to rescue Maclean before the net closed on him ... two ideas merged: Burgess's return to London and the rescue of Maclean.

138

Not only did Maclean need to be rescued, but so did Burgess. One evening in the home of CIA officer Kermit Roosevelt, Burgess got so drunk that he 'boasted of his Soviet connections'.[18] The next morning while Roosevelt was reporting to Dulles, (who had also received a report from Angleton) Burgess fled. He had engineered his recall to London by obtaining three speeding tickets within two days, and assaulting a traffic policeman. Burgess then travelled on the *Queen Mary* back to London. During the voyage he met an American medical student who also worked for the CIA. He had been watching Burgess, and remained in contact with him after his arrival in England. The FBI, CIA and the British Security Service knew about Burgess and Maclean being Soviet agents; both of whom feared being arrested. But the British authorities had no intention of arresting the duo. Clumsy surveillance was made to alert the two. Then, just prior to the Foreign Secretary authorizing their apprehension, Burgess received a telephone call from Blunt advising both Burgess and Maclean to vanish via an escape route partly organized by RIS officer Vladimir Petrov. They travelled by a rented car to Southampton, and at the dockside was a Special Branch officer standing by: if not to wave Burgess and Maclean goodbye, then at least to watch their departure. Upon their arrival in France, they spent their weekend with the American medical student. One can say that the duo were 'escorted' all the way to the Soviet bloc by various Western security services. It was not until headlines in the press in February 1956 that the world learned that Burgess and Maclean had been long-term Soviet agents.

One person who was not surprised was Lord Vansittart, who, following the defection of Burgess and Maclean, repeated charges that the British government had 'permitted various important agencies to become honeycombed with Communists', and added that: 'according to Belgrade Radio, four officers of our secret service based in Cairo during the war were Communists and went into Yugoslavia on various missions.[19] The first, Major Peter Wright, was until 1947 our military attaché in

Belgrade. Another, Betty Wallace, belongs to the leadership of the CP which has just revealed that she is now in France on a mission connected with the current strikes in that country. Another, Kenneth Shyers, recently published an official study for our Eastern affairs bureau. The fourth, James Klugman, is the editor of a Communist periodical and the electoral agent of Harry Pollitt.'[20]

Across in Washington, Philby was nearing the end of his time in the capital. During his time as SIS liaison officer with the CIA, he had, in the words of the former CIA officer, Wilbur Crane Eveland, 'figuratively speaking, the keys to the CIA's safes'. His knowledge enabled the Soviets to learn about joint CIA-SIS operations in Germany, Poland (as head of Section IX Philby had networks in Yugoslavia and Poland put at his disposal), Albania, the Ukraine and China. Both SIS and CIA files about the joint operations in China remain totally closed. However, the author has obtained details about other Western operations into China that indicates the form that the joint CIA-SIS operations took.

Following the Communist victory in China, thousands of anti-Communists fled. By 1954 French Indo-China contained 25,000 Chinese refugees and North Burma contained 30,000 of them. It was called 'The Iron Triangle'. Many of the 55,000 men became anti-Communist guerrillas, trained by Chiang Kai-shek's 4th Army in Formosa. The guerrillas and would-be insurgents were moved into the south of China via Kwangsi province, ruled by the war-lord Si Taung-jen, former President of China. Liaison man for the operation was the ex-OSS officer Hillaire du Berrier, who established contact between Si Taung-jen and the French military, who had proposed the operation. The guerrillas made deep inroads; they contacted the underground in China. To prove that they had actually visited certain areas, they returned with cinema tickets – they also returned, in the words of one former security officer, 'with blood on their hands'.[21]

Interestingly enough, the CIA did not like the idea of the

China operation. Perhaps their attitude had something to do with the previous operations, of which Philby was cognizant. The joint CIA-SIS operations which Philby learned of were the last ones he heard about whilst officially an SIS officer. He was not to (officially) remain an SIS officer much longer. Just as the FBI and CIA knew about Burgess and Maclean being Soviet agents, they also knew the same about Philby. General Bedell Smith, Director of the CIA, wrote an ultimatum to the British authorities: 'Fire Philby, or we break off the intelligence relationship.' He also made it clear in a tough, angry letter to Sir Stuart Menzies that Philby had to leave America and that he was no longer acceptable to the CIA as an SIS linkman. After all, the CIA had enough evidence to sink Philby, from information gained by Angleton and cryptographers who had intercepted Russian messages which contained information about Philby's activities for the USSR.

On 11 June 1951, the Director-General of the Security Service, Sir Percy Sillitoe, flew to Washington for consultations with Hoover, Bedell Smith and Dulles. Had Sillitoe failed at first to grasp what Philby had to do with the matter of Burgess and Maclean, Hoover obligingly enlightened him. The three American officials were unanimous: Philby had to go. Philby duly received a terse wire from Menzies, summoning him to return home to London. He flew back unescorted and could have taken this opportunity to escape and defect. However, he did not do so. Upon arriving in London, he went directly to the SIS HQ in Broadway, and was met there by Commander Jack Easton, the Assistant Chief of SIS. Easton told Philby that the Security Service officer Dick White wanted to see him immediately. Both met, and during the preliminary session, Philby denied knowing Maclean and claimed that he had been completely fooled by Burgess. Neither White nor Arthur Martin were impressed by the interview, and a second interview was arranged a few days later, which proved to be as inconclusive as the first. Later, Philby said that he 'was not surprised to receive a summons from the Chief. He had told me that he had received a strong letter[22] from Bedell Smith, the terms of which precluded any possibility of my returning to Washington ... the Chief called me a second time and told me, with obvious distress, that he would have to ask for my resignation. He would be generous: £4,000 in lieu of pension.'

Menzies had been totally against any interrogation of Philby. One is therefore not surprised to learn that both Menzies and Philby viewed with trepidation a forthcoming judicial enquiry, over the circumstances of the Burgess-Maclean escape, in the hands of H. J. P. Milmo KC, who had worked for the Security Service during the war. According to Philby:

> The mention of Milmo indicated that a crisis was at hand. I knew him and of him. He was a skilled interrogator; he was the man MI5 usually brought in for the kill. As I drove with the Chief across St James's Park to Leconfield House [MI5 HQ], I braced myself for a sticky ordeal.

Still, Philby need not have worried because certain old SIS friends protected him. Former SIS officer and Tory MP Dick Brooman-White together with Tim Milne totally defended Philby, as did (Sir) Richard Clarke. Indeed, the Chief of SIS did not, unlike the Security Service, believe him to be guilty.

Before the secret trial began, evidence was gathered against Philby concerning his salary whilst he was First Secretary in America. The salary was between £950 and £1,250 per annum, but some colleagues estimated that he must have been spending at least £7,000 per annum. They also gathered evidence of his association with Burgess and Maclean and the US intercepts. When questioned by Milmo, Philby was able to deny him the confession which he required as a lawyer. Suddenly Milmo gave up, and was replaced by William Skardon, who in the words of Philby 'was far more dangerous than the ineffective White or the blustering Milmo'. It was Skardon who had trapped and caught Fuchs.

Once again Philby need not have worried: SIS prevented

Skardon (who would have worked on Philby for months) from asking properly put questions. Skardon was told to suspend his enquiries. According to one former security officer 'extraordinary attempts were made to protect Philby'. During one interrogation, Philby defended his actions by declaring that he had been posing as a 'double' agent for several years, with full permission from SIS. In fact, Philby had been given permission to play the part of a 'double' agent with the Russians: to approach them and to pretend that he was ready to work for them. Naturally his British chiefs had no idea that Philby actually had been for years a real RIS agent, when as head of Section IX, he approached the Soviets to be a 'double' agent.

Now the enquiries were over, and officially Philby was out of SIS, but despite this, he was still employed by SIS and worked in Cyprus and other places – whilst being watched. In the opinion of a former SOE officer, stated to the author: 'He must have been a "double" agent after 1951 for if there's the slightest doubt about anyone, he's out.' But Philby was not out: he was still in. That he was in, and because SIS considered Philby to be 'theirs' explains why Sir Maurice Oldfield considered that 'Kim felt justified in doing what he did'. Obviously, because he had permission to be a 'double' agent. No doubt the Soviets let Philby have some information for SIS which they could afford to give away, even if it meant losing a few expendable agents in 'the field', to bolster Philby's role as an SIS officer working against Russia. Philby certainly fooled SIS into believing that he was 100 per cent on the British side. It took, according to Sir Dick White (Deputy-General, the Security Service) until 1955 to be 'definitely known' that Philby was, in fact 100 per cent working for the Russians. In the meantime, from 1951 to 1956, Philby, according to an American military intelligence official, 'did more damage to British-American relations after he came under suspicion than he ever achieved while his cover was still secure [up to 1951]'. This damage, as we shall see later, was why the CIA forced Philby to flee from Beirut.

143

Philby's association with various parts of American intelligence organizations began during World War II when he was involved with setting up the American Office of Strategic Services under General Donovan. This developed, after the war, eventually into the CIA which Philby also helped to set up. In the Middle East, he splashed around far more money than he would have received from the British or the Russians. Only the CIA paid an agent so liberally. Unlike the FBI which has released 3,196 pages about Philby, Burgess and Maclean, the CIA has released only a handful of uninformative pages about Philby. His relationship with the CIA lasted for fifteen years. As the major and senior intelligence organization in the British-American partnership, the CIA had a major say in what happened to Philby. We know that the CIA in 1951 demanded that he be recalled from Washington and fired – this duly happened. When he went to Beirut in 1956, ostensibly as a journalist, the CIA, at the very least, knew about this move, but did not veto the idea. During his time in the Middle East, Philby and his travels were watched by CIA officers, including Miles Copeland who considered that Philby had visited too many places for too few journalistic results. He was also observed by Wilbur Crane Eveland who, during the crucial days prior to Philby's defection from Beirut, was virtually holding Philby's hand.

After 1951 the Soviets became suspicious of Philby because they were not sure where his loyalty lay. It was of vital importance to them to know whether or not Philby was reliable and was totally on their side. Consequently, the RIS thoroughly questioned Dr Otto John, who in 1954 had crossed from West Berlin into the Eastern bloc, in order to determine that vital question. During World War II, John was an Abwehr officer who supplied reports to the British. His reports were refused by Philby, including one about the July 1944 generals' plot against Hitler. Another one of Stalin's nightmares was that a secret agreement would be reached between the Western powers and the German resistance. Had Britain followed up the peace feelers, John would have undoubtedly made Philby's acquaintance since he was responsible for Spain and Portugal. John had told the RIS that all of the peace feelers had failed – and he never mentioned Philby's name. The RIS were convinced that Philby had not been going behind their backs and that they could rely upon him. This conviction was reached in late 1954.

In the meantime, rumours had been floating around the British Parliament and Fleet Street (as known by the writer Cyril Connolly who had known Burgess and Maclean before they defected) about Philby being the 'third man'. Across in America, FBI Chief, J. Edgar Hoover, was convinced that Philby was the 'third man', and wanted to do his utmost to expose him. Former FBI agent Bill Harvey, now the CIA Station Chief in Berlin, 'blew' Philby when he provided information to local journalists. Word eventually reached the *Sunday News* in New York, and its edition on 23 October actually named Philby. The publication of this news enabled Jack Fisherman, the editor of the *Empire News* (London) who had been sniffing around the 'third man' story, to persuade the Labour MP for Brixton, Lieutenant-Colonel Marcus Lipton to raise a question in the House of Commons the following Tuesday afternoon:

> Has the Prime Minister made up his mind to cover up at all costs the dubious third man activities of Mr Harold Philby who was First Secretary at the Washington Embassy a little while ago; and is he determined to stifle all discussion on the very great matters which were evaded in the wretched White Paper [about Burgess and Maclean] which is an insult to the intelligence of the country?

Soon after the Prime Minister received a brief which was totally at variance with the views of the FBI and CIA; and on November Harold Macmillan read his brief in Parliament. The crucial part said:

> No evidence has been found that Philby was responsible for warning Burgess or Maclean. While in Government service he carried out his

145

duties ably and conscientiously. I have no reason to conclude that Mr Philby has at any time betrayed the interests of this country, or to identify him with the so-called 'third man', if indeed, there was one.

Philby was therefore cleared; and within twelve months he was sent by SIS to Beirut for just over six years, as covered in chapters 8 to 10. Whilst he was in Beirut he was watched by the British, the CIA and the Israelis. Details of the British surveillance are hidden behind an official secrets screen. However, the author has discovered two examples: opposite Philby's apartment lived Mr and Mrs Cook. Mr Cook was an SIS-employed journalist. He observed Philby's apartment and saw his 'comings and goings'.[23] On a visit to the Lebanon in April 1962 F. W. D. Deakin, a fellow Westminster schoolboy, a former British officer and a First Warden of the SIS-linked St Anthony's College, Oxford, spent a long evening with Philby 'and remembers how reluctant Kim was to leave, how anxious to cling to someone familiar, how near to collapse'.[24] Posted to Beirut was CIA officer Miles Copeland, who was instructed to watch Philby. 'We'll pay the expenses involved in doing so'[25] he was told by the CIA. Copeland told the author how 'Philby was observed sending messages'. He had been seen doing so by an agent of Colonel Tewfik Jalbout, 'a trusted ally of the American CIA',[26] who saw Philby one night on the terrace of his apartment waving a dark object to and fro in the air. Two nights later, using a pair of polaroid glasses, the police security man observed Philby once again waving some object in various directions and it was possible to see that he was sending 'black light' messages. The recipient of the signals could have been one of several hundred people. However, a search by the police narrowed it down to two or three suspects, one of them an Armenian, believed to be a Soviet agent, but there was not sufficient evidence to make an arrest. Not surprisingly, because the whole story was CIA disinformation. On a separate occasion, one of Jalbout's detectives observed Philby twice changing taxi cabs and eventually arriving at a small sweetshop owned by an Armenian in the city. Shortly afterwards, the Soviet military attaché entered the shop. No arrests followed, because once again the allegations were CIA disinformation.

During this period the Israelis had been busy looking into Philby's earlier life. Apart from the information provided by Teddy Kollek, as mentioned earlier in this chapter, the brilliant Israeli officer, Ellie Cohen, had discovered that Philby had actually visited, via Turkey, the Soviet Union.

Following his arrest in 1962. Blake revealed a piece of information concerning one of the complex operations in which both he and Philby were both involved, that pointed indubitably at the truth; Philby was a Soviet agent. Additionally, the Soviet defectors, Michael Goleniewski and Anatoliy Golitsyn, (the latter was code-named KAGO) informed the CIA that Philby was a Soviet agent. The CIA informed SIS who considered that Philby had been 'blown'. Action had to be taken.

In the late spring of 1962, Tim Milne, a long-time friend and supporter of Philby, visited him in Beirut. Milne made no progress, although he charged Philby as being a Soviet agent. All his visit did was to alert Philby to the fact that he had been betrayed and might need to take some action about it. Aside from conferring with his Soviet controller, Yuri Modin, who visited Beirut in May 1962, Philby decided to stay in Beirut: after all, he had very good sources of income, and could become drunk as often as he wanted to.

Had the British authorities wanted to arrest Philby, and return him to England for trial, this could very easily have been done. For example, in October when he passed through the British colony of Aden into North Yemen, he could have been arrested, but was not. Instead he was given 'red carpet' treatment as observed by the veteran foreign correspondent Edward Behr. Both flew into Cairo together during the time when the net was slowly closing around Philby. At Cairo airport, whilst Behr battled for a taxi to take him to his hotel, he noticed that Philby was met by a British Embassy car; and for the duration of the trip was the honoured guest of a high Embassy official.

SIS did not want Philby returned to England because of the embarrassment it would have caused them and the government. And so, they were left with a handful of choices. Firstly liquidate Philby; secondly offer him an immunity from prosecution, and turn him from a Soviet agent into a British agent (which is what we shall see happened to Blunt); or lastly, force him to defect. Option one was discounted for it could have lead to a 'tit for tat' situation with the RIS. Option two was acted upon in terms of Nicholas Elliott, also an old friend of Philby, going to Beirut just before Christmas and confronting him. Elliott told Philby that there was no doubt of his guilt and offered an immunity provided he confessed his past. Philby agreed, and partially revealed his work for the RIS. The following evening Philby produced a two-page typewritten document which he signed. Elliott then flew direct from Beirut to Washington to brief James Jesus Angleton. 'Perhaps the CIA,' explained a former SOE officer to the author, 'had had enough of Philby, and demanded "get rid of him".' From that point on the CIA in Beirut certainly watched him. One day, Kermit Roosevelt observed that 'he [Philby] got quite drunk on a yacht in the harbour and fell off the deck into the water. But drunk or not, he never said a wrong word or gave away anything'.[27] Wilbur Crane Eveland 'talked with him a few days earlier [before he defected]'.[28] On the evening of 23 January 1963, although due to attend a dinner party, Philby suddenly defected, leaving the Lebanon for the USSR.

Espionage writers have wondered why Philby suddenly bolted from Beirut. The reason is quite simple: he feared being killed. After the CIA discovered that he was betraying American officers and agents, it was decided he should be 'rubbed out if the British would not take any action'.[29] There was a contract to eliminate him. 'He was told the CIA had a hit team in Beirut to bump him off. There wasn't. It was enough to make him clear off.'[30] He was warned by another SIS officer who has since retired from the Service, with a CMG.

It has been said that his defection spurred the Security Service into looking for other RIS agents. This they had been doing anyway. In addition to providing conclusive evidence of Philby's treachery, Golitsyn gave leads about six other penetrations. One of the men implicated was Blunt. Blunt accepted the offer of immunity, and provided information. Others found to have been involved, directly or peripherally, with the RIS were given the choice of being tried for treason, or receiving an immunity from prosecution (as did one of the Galbraiths who was associated with Vassall), continuing their lives as British agents – this time against rather than for the Russians, 'or being dealt with – and in some cases that meant being killed'.[31] Some of those who refused to be 'turned', once their Soviet role was discovered, shortly afterwards died, in a series of 'mysterious deaths'.[32]

Richard Brooman-White who, since their time together in Section Five, was a life-long friend of Philby. He was a distinctly High Tory, and subsequently became MP for Rutherglen. From this lofty perch, he both protected, supported and used his political influence on Philby's behalf. He died on 23 January 1964.

Tom Wyllie, a favourite drinking 'companion' of Burgess, was known in the Foreign Office for the wild parties he gave during his period as Resident Clerk. He and Burgess in 1936 made an extensive tour of the Third Reich gathering impressions, which they later energetically disseminated in England. He died in the winter of 1964.

Thomas Harris was ideologically the same as Philby. Indeed he recommended Philby for Section Five (headed by Richard Brooman-White) within which he was employed dealing with so-called 'double' agents (German agents, for example, who had been turned into British agents, but Germany did not know that, so that at the appropriate time, the turned agents were able to feed important misinformation or disinformation back to Germany). He was killed in January 1964 in a car crash in Majorca. The police could find nothing wrong with the car.

By comparison, officer 'X', unlike the aforementioned, agreed to be 'turned', and continued to hold a top post in counter-espionage. His usefulness to both America and British counter-espionage ended in the late 1960s. Within a few days after his official retirement, he was rewarded with a fatal heart attack.

Confirmation about Blunt's role as a Soviet agent was provided in 1964 by an American citizen, Michael Straight, who had been recruited by Blunt whilst at Cambridge in the mid-1930s. Not only did he 'blow' Blunt, as a recruiter for the RIS, but Straight also provided the Security Service with the names of at least 150 other people, of whom 30 to 40 have lived as 'moles' becoming members of the Labour Party, becoming barristers and judges. There were other 'moles' in public life, indeed one or two at the Foreign Office, the Home Office and the Treasury. The 'moles' according to Straight, were not Soviet agents. (But they were 'in place' and could have been activated by the Soviets at any time.) In 1983 Straight confirmed that there was a Fifth man, a Sixth man and a Seventh man.

Following Blunt's and Straight's revelations, a large-scale investigation was initiated by the Security Service. A team was headed by Tony Motion, who discovered that the Russian espionage network at Cambridge had been far wider than was generally thought. Many of the people Motion investigated had become household names, and the influence of these people, after being discovered as RIS agents, was neutralized, having been internally dealt with by the Service. Other people were so rich and powerful that nothing could be done, as in the case of 'the Lord'. There was simply not the legal proof to take action. As one former security officer remarked to the author: 'the ultimately answerable would go, perhaps with greater caution, on their chosen way'.

Within two years of being in the USSR, Philby was stripped of his Order of the British Empire. In the meantime, he had been writing *My Silent War*. Prior to its publication in Britain in 1968, the British authorities obtained a copy. They were highly concerned because the book revealed details about major intelligence security operations, organizations and identities of key officers. Publication had to be stopped. The Attorney-General, (the now) Baron Elwyn Jones (and the only Attorney-General between 1964 and 1974 who was not informed about the decision to give an immunity to Blunt) should have stopped publication. However, (for reasons best known to himself) Jones, a former Trinity man, did not curtail publication.

Until the publication of this book, Philby's 'hidden years' have remained hidden. As mentioned in the previous chapter, Philby explained that '[my] experiences in the Middle East from 1956 to 1963 do not lend themselves to narrative form'. So, he was at great pains to conceal the facts about them. In this book we have lifted the curtain somewhat. Total access would have required simultaneous access to the files of the American, British and Soviet intelligence services. Nevertheless, of these years, they are not now so hidden, especially during his time in the Middle East, showing that, unlike as postulated by some writers, Philby was not a washed-out, washed-up and retired SIS officer and RIS agent. We know that he was an effective agent whose information was used by the Soviets to a deadly effect, and whose influence had an adverse effect on British policy in that region.

This chapter has also covered Philby's career in the Soviet Union since 1983. He may have remained active to the end. He, as suggested by a former assistant Vice-Chief of SIS '[was] occasionally brought to Moscow by the RIS to confront and embarrass American visitors who had former CIA connections'.[33] This suggestion, naturally, was laughed at when mentioned to a former CIA officer.

Uninformed press reports in 1983 suggested that Philby had, retired. Knowledgeable sources suggested otherwise. The two-timing Russian officer Vitaly Yerchenko worked with both Philby and Blake immediately before his defection to the West in 1985. And Washington CIA sources have claimed that Philby might have masterminded Yerchenko's 'defection' to the West and return to the Russians. Said one source: 'It certainly has the Philby stamp with all the twists and plots that he loves', which he employed when head of the Anti-Soviet Section during the latter war years.

Philby and his circle remain deeply embodied in the British psyche, a reminder of cataclysmic treachery and betrayals never to be forgotten or forgiven. On the other hand, some former members of SIS damn him on another basis, the class basis. As Nicholas Elliott explained to the former CIA officer, Miles Copeland: 'He let down our class.'[34] This meant more to Elliott than anything else he had done. After all, he had let down the British 'ruling class'.

13

ENDGAME

From 1971, when Philby in *Kodumaa* exposed the identities of SIS officers, real or alleged agents, and SIS operatives in the Middle East, he remained unobtrusive in terms of not being interviewed by the Western media, or quoted, until November 1987. That month, in a Moscow TV broadcast, he claimed that 'the West was fomenting unrest [in Latvia]'[1] and denounced 'Western interference in the Baltic'. Philby further alleged how the West used 'Latvian nationalists to sow dissension in the Soviet Union',[2] and were 'CIA manipulated'. On the other hand, US intelligence sources alleged that the TV broadcast was 'intended to read as a threat to increase Soviet destabilizations in the West'.[3] Therefore, according to your own political perspective, you make up your own mind as to who was factual, or not.

Philby, obviously, was being employed by the RIS for propaganda and intelligence purposes, be his allegations true or not. Yet, at the same time our 'Kim' reportedly expressed a desire and a hankering for a last look at England. The following month, Tory MP (and espionage writer) Rupert Allason tabled a question which asked for an assurance that the government would not give Philby an immunity from, prosecution for treason in the event of his visiting Britain. The Attorney General Sir Patrick Mayhew, concurred. Later, Philby subsequently described his alleged desire to visit England as 'a rumour which apparently started in Canada of all places...'[4]

In December 1987 a most bizarre 'exclusive' appeared in the *Star*. It claimed that Philby had 'ditched his fifth wife' and had 'gone off to finish his days among bubbly blondes in Latvia'. The most outrageous assertion was that Philby was 'worried more and more about British intelligence [SIS] tracking him down in Moscow'.[5] But for years the SIS, via Graham Greene[6] and other former officers knew his address. A month later Philby was photographed with his fifth wife by British reporter at their Moscow apartment. The whole of the *Star* article appeared to have been 'planted' or 'placed' in order to try and 'spook' Philby for whatever reasons British officialdom had at that time.

The British reporter who photographed Philby was Phillip Knightley, who for over twenty years, since he co-authored a book about Philby in 1968, had corresponded with Philby, and had hoped to meet him. By seeing Philby in his Moscow apartment over a period of days–the first Western journalist to do so – Knightley had a major scoop, which it is believed he capitalized upon to the tune of half a million pounds. The *Sunday Times*, 20 March, headlined: 'WORLD EXCLUSIVE: FIRST INTERVIEW WITH THE MASTERSPY WHO BETRAYED BRITAIN'. However, aside from providing details about Philby's life in Moscow, the published articles provided little new, if anything at all, about his espionage career. As Chapman Pincher observed: 'There's nothing new [in the articles].'[7]

Following the serialization in the *Sunday Times* about Philby a CIA team at Langley sifted through Philby's remarks to Knightley and along with other US intelligence agencies reached the following conclusions:

On 10 April, the London *Sunday Times* published the last instalment of Phillip Knightley's interviews with HAR 'Kim' Philby, the notorious British traitor and Soviet mole who penetrated the highest echelon of the United Kingdom's Secret Intelligence Service. These

154

interviews were significant for a number of reasons. One was the subject; Mr Philby was arguably, the most successful spy of this century. Another was the amount of information – and disinformation – that he provided in their course. But most important was the fact that they appeared to signal a reversal of the Soviet Union's long-standing policy against the extensive interview of Western traitors and defectors to whom it had granted asylum.

The events of the following two months seemed to confirm this assessment. On 17 April, the *Washington Post* printed a summary of Ronald Kessler's interview with Karl Koecher, a Czechoslovakian intelligence officer who had penetrated the Agency [the CIA]. Six days later George Blake, a former senior official of the British Foreign Ministry [meaning the SIS], surfaced for the first time in 18 years, appearing on the Soviet television programme 'Before and After Midnight'. And on 23 May, *Newsweek* magazine published an account of an interview with CIA turn-coat Edward Lee Howard, whose disclosures reportedly destroyed the Agency's 'Moscow Station'.

This sudden reversal of Soviet policy concerning the interview of Soviet agents and intelligence officers is puzzling for two reasons. First, because it constitutes such a radical departure from past Soviet practices, and second, because it is so entirely inconsistent with the Soviet Union's obsessive preoccupation with secrecy, a characteristic that is especially pronounced in intelligence and intelligence-related matters.

One possible explanation is that glasnost has finally penetrated the Soviet intelligence/internal security apparat. Another is that the RIS has surfaced this particular rogues' gallery of traitors and spies for some specific operational purpose. But it is more likely still that the true explanation combines the major elements of both. Assuming that this assessment is correct, the questions as to what type of operation the Soviets have mounted and what objective, or objectives, they hope to accomplish remain to be answered.

On the basis of the evidence available, two types of operations suggest themselves. The first is a political operation designed to influence public opinion and political behavior in the United Kingdon and/or the United States. The second is a counter-intelligence operation, ie, an offensive action, against the intelligence services of one or both of these countries.

If the operation is political, there are obvious benefits to be gained

155

from the surfacing of Messrs. Philby, Koecher, Blake and Howard. Of these, the most important is the establishment of an RIS-controlled back-channel to the Western mass media.

Because the interviewing of these men dispelled much of the sinister mystery that has surrounded them, they can now be represented as ordinary men who, when forced to choose, chose 'socialism' over 'capitalism'. Their demons thus exorcized, they can now be exploited to shape Western public opinion in ways that no Soviet could. They can, for example, lend the appearance of substance to the Soviet Union's peculiar claim of moral equivalence to the Western democracies. Or they can embarrass their former governments by purveying information designed to discomfort them.

If, on the other hand, the operation is a counter-intelligence effort, other but equally great benefits may be obtained. First and foremost among these is the likely success of a pre-emptive attack upon the recently created American counter-intelligence centre in the Agency. One particularly promising form of attack would be the public ridicule of Western intelligence services by traitors and Soviet agents.

At first glance this appears absurd or at the very least counter-productive. By flaunting their past successes in penetrating the Agency, the Soviets would only strengthen the resolve of American policy-makers to prevent future penetrations. This, however, may be precisely the point.

Because the establishment of an American counter-intelligence centre cannot now be stopped, the Soviet intelligence apparat cannot prevent its eventual operation. It can, however, attempt to shape it in the way least threatening to Soviet intelligence interests. Specifically, it can exploit American sensitivity to penetration to skew its priorities away from offensive operations and toward defensive efforts. Given the current climate within the intelligence community and the general confusion surrounding the subject of counter-intelligence, it is difficult to avoid the conclusion that such an effort would stand a remarkably good chance of success.

As attractive as this opportunity must be, there is no reason to believe that it is any more alluring than the political opportunities described earlier. In the absence of compelling evidence, then, it is impossible to render any substantial judgement as to whether the operation that the Soviets are mounting is a political or counter-intelligence operation. It could be either; but more likely it is both.

Although such speculation is probably premature, it is supported by some scant evidence. The first is the fact that while the interviews of Messrs. Koecher and Howard were released more or less coincidentally with those of Messrs. Philby and Blake, they were both taken approximately a year earlier [in April and June of 1987, respectively]. The second is that the construction of complex operations designed to achieve categorically different objectives is an operational trademark of the RIS. Known as kombinatsiya, this tactic joins diverse activities separated by time and space to enhance overall operational results. In practice, kombinatsiya has proved to be a devastating weapon when wielded against the free and open societies of the West.

Whatever the actual case may be, the developing operation, like all hostile operations, is best defended by aggressive counter-intelligence actions. Unfortunately, however, the United States virtually dismantled its counter-intelligence capability between 1973 and 1975 when the Agency's centralized counter-intelligence programme was effectively terminated. As a result, the United States no longer possesses the means to satisfactorily determine the true nature of the threat posed by this developing Soviet operation or the capability to adequately counter it.

Given this unfortunate situation, the United States has little choice but to make the assumption that the Soviet operation is directed against its most vulnerable asset – the fledgling counter-intelligence centre – and mobilize all available resources to defend it. Although these resources are for the most part intellectual rather than material, the net effect is much the same: Scarce resources are still diverted, thus increasing the danger to other possible targets.

Such a strategy is so fraught with danger that it can only be justified by extreme circumstances. Unfortunately, this is precisely the case. Circumstances are extreme and they are not likely to soon improve. Despite the promise of a new counter-intelligence center, there is as yet no assurance that budgetary constraints will permit it to be properly structured, staffed, or supported. And even if it is, it will still require a lengthy period of time to gain the necessary institutional knowledge, experience, and skill to become truly effective.[8]

Following the *Sunday Times*'s serialization about Philby, the former CIA officer, Miles Copeland and an SIS expert on Philby met at Copeland's home over the Easter weekend, and came to the conclusion that Philby had been actualizing RIS 'disinformation designed to sow dissension between the US and Britain [read the CIA and SIS]'.[9]

Philby's actualizing of RIS disinformation did not last much longer, for he died on 11 May at the age of 76 in Moscow. His death was not mourned by certain former SIS officers. As one former officer commented: 'I will have to open a bottle of champagne. I am delighted with the news and I hope he died in the greatest agony in light of the agony he caused other people.'[10] Another officer added: 'I hope he died in agony and that he got his just deserves. Nobody is going to have very happy feelings for a man who betrayed people and friendships.'[11] The Soviet agent's death came 'not a moment to soon' said wartime SIS colleague Robert Cecil. 'He was the most dangerous of them all. Philby gave away so many agents. He was running them into the Soviet territory. They were all picked up and massacred.'[12]

On 14 May Philby was buried with full military honours in a military cemetery not far from the country dacha where he had lived. In attendance was his wife Rufina, and his son John.

Following the death of Philby the mass media, once again, poured out its own version of his motivation, and the West's fascination in Philby. Perhaps the best account of his fascination came from Phillip Knightley:

The truth is that treachery is an elastic concept and in Philby's case has more to do with betrayal of class interests than with betrayal of country. No one pretends that if Philby had been the son of an accountant, a grey recruit from a north London grammar school and a red brick university, treachery would still be under discussion nearly half a century later. No, the fascination in Philby lies not in his act of betrayal but in who he was and why he did it. The enigma is that he was a pillar of the establishment he was supposed to be protecting. George Blake, said to have sent more agents to their deaths, does not hold the same interest because he was not part of the ruling class in the first place, whereas if Mrs Thatcher had been around in Philby's day to ask if he were 'one of us' the answer would have been a resounding yes. Even worse, Philby betrayed for no material gain. As Sir Robert Mackenzie said when I told him in 1967 that we were writing a book on Philby, 'Make it clear – and this is important – that Philby didn't sell his country's secrets. He gave them away. He didn't do it for money. He never got a penny. He did it for his ideals.'[13]

APPENDIX

ROTHSCHILD – THE FIRST MAN

Here, extracted from a 1988 issue of *The Lobster*, a periodical devoted to intelligence and political matters, is an article about Lord Victor Rothschild, who, according to an American intelligence organization 'is correctly viewed by counter-intelligence experts as part of the "Circle of 25" that included Soviet agents Kim Philby, Guy Burgess, Anthony Blunt and Donald Maclean.'[1]

ROTHSCHILD, PHILBY, THE RIGHT AND THE FIRST MAN

We understand that Lord Rothschild was badly shaken last year [1987] by the many innuendoes linking him to the Cambridge spy ring of the 1930s. A typical example was Anthony Glees's book on 'British Intelligence and Communist Subversion':

> Rothschild [was] remarkably intimate with people subsequently proven to be secret Communists, and Blunt was a major Communist mole.[2]

160

In a gesture of loyalty, one of his old 'pupils', Robin Butler, now the Cabinet Secretary, organized a reunion dinner of the 1970s Think Tank in December 1986 in order to cheer up the ageing *éminence grise*. Not long afterwards Rothschild sent his extraordinary letter to the *Daily Telegraph*:

> Since at least 1980 up to present time there have been innuendoes in the press to the effect that I am 'the Fifth Man', in other words a Soviet agent. The Director-General of MI5 should state publicly that he had unequivocal, repeat, unequivocal evidence, that I am not, and have never been a Soviet agent.[3]

It was a bizarre letter if only for the fact that it is impossible to prove such a negative. The Prime Minister's reply offered no such proof:

> I am advised that we have no evidence that he was ever a Soviet agent.[4]

This bland statement made no mention of the 'unequivocal evidence' Rothschild had demanded, and only served to make the episode even more mysterious. Chapman Pincher, acting as the unofficial spokesman for Rothschild, wrote: 'The Prime Minister's statement on Friday will not fully satisfy him.'[5]

In his book *Molehunt* Nigel West deals with the accusations against Rothschild, though much was apparently cut by the libel lawyers. Without mentioning Rothschild's references to the innuendoes starting in 1980, West writes:

> Yet strangely, it was later to be claimed by Pincher that 'people were suggesting that Rothschild himself had been a spy'. [A Soviet agent.] He also reported [Peter] Wright as stating that 'articles had been suggesting that Rothschild had been a Soviet agent himself'. In fact no such articles ever appeared...[6]

In fact there were veiled references. A jokey piece in the 'Londoner's Diary' in the *Evening Standard* following the exposure of Anthony Blunt said that 'Rothschild himself is known among the cognoscenti as the First Man'.[7]

Following the Prime Minister's statement, the whispers might have ceased had not Rothschild himself unwittingly – and so far unnoticed by the media – reopened the whole question of his relationship to the Cambridge Comintern in March 1987. In the *Daily Express* he refuted the suggestion that he and 'Kim' Philby had been friends, stating that 'he had met Philby once only'.[8] Really? It would appear that somebody had been lying for a number of years.

In his book on Philby, *The Third Man*, E. H. Cookridge wrote:

> During his first two years at Trinity, Kim Philby had remained inconspicuous. To his natural shyness he added a self-imposed restraint, a strange secretiveness, which he preserved even with the few close friends he had made. Amongst them were ... Victor Rothschild, afterwards the third baron, a brilliant biochemist, who became a daring intelligence officer during the war.[9]

Cookridge adds:

> His [Rothschild's] war work brought him in contact with Kim Philby who was in charge of the Iberian section of SIS at the time when Lord Rothschild was concentrating with the detection of ship sabotage occurring at Gibraltar ... Lord Rothschild ... remained for several months in Gibraltar ... Kim Philby paid several visits to the Rock at that time.[10]

Anthony Boyle, in his *The Climate of Treason*, notes another encounter between Rothschild and Philby:

> It was in Paris during the bleak winter of 1955–56, when Philby was busily forming his new Soviet counter-espionage section, that Muggeridge met him again ... Two small incidents imprinted themselves indelibly on Muggeridge's mind. Each concerned Philby. The first was a heated discussion at table about the rights and

wrongs of withholding important Bletchley intercepts from the Soviet Union. It was Victor Rothschild who raised the matter, startling Muggeridge by his vehemence in criticising this standard practice ... The debate waxed hotter, and, for once, Philby joined in...[11]

And finally, Philby himself, during the series of interviews he did with Phillip Knightley for the *Sunday Times* recalled meeting Rothschild after the war:

> In 1946 he [Rothschild] told me that he had decided to keep copies of the MI5 card indexes of some people he thought might be security risks. Then Rothschild said to me: 'And how long have you been a member of the party, Kim?' And I said, 'Me, Victor?' And Rothschild said, 'Just a little joke. I try it on everyone.'[12]

The evidence shows that Rothschild knew and met with Philby – before, during and after the war. It may be that Philby was leaving one last bomb in Rothschild's path. But Philby did explode the potential threat by claiming that there was no Comintern cell at Cambridge – and, consequently, no 'Fifth Man'. Instead, he replaced it with a 'First Man', Professor Maurice Dobbs, the original talent-spotter. Dobbs seems a fairly logical choice and fits in with the evidence Philby has already provided.[13] However, there is one important dissenter from the idea of Dobbs as the 'First Man', namely Michael Straight, the man who had blown Blunt. Following the *Sunday Times* interviews with Philby, Straight told the *Sunday Express*, 'Philby is using the name of a dead man to cover up for someone else.'[14]

Who?

In his fiction book on Philby *The Other Side of Silence*, spy-writer Ted Allbeury calls him 'Milord'.

> 'And who recruited him for the Soviets?'
> 'I'm sure he was looked over by "Milord" who had already

spotted Burgess and Maclean. At that stage I should think that Burgess was the man who mattered. I'd say too that Philby got his Soviet funds through Burgess.' [He did whilst he was in Spain.]

'What was "Milord" doing at the time?'

'Teaching science at Cambridge. The details will be on your files.'[15]

It just so happens that Rothschild taught science at Cambridge. According to the Right the 'First Man', the 'original source of evil – the original seducer', is Lord Victor Rothschild. And the evidence is contained in 'an ultra-secret British government [Cabinet Office] file'.[16] Kenneth de Courcy, a man who pops up constantly in anti-Communist politics of the last fifty years, believes 'Milord' to have been Rothschild. In September 1963 de Courcy wrote a remarkable series of letters.[17]

I am, alas correct in my fears. An entire network of Russian agents has [illegible] since the thirties. Rothschild played a major role in recruiting them in the belief that Russia was necessary to defeat Nazi Germany – or rather it was his belated excuse because Hitler had not risen to power when Rothschild started. I suppose he argued he saw it coming. His puppets were Burgess and co...

My prime concern is its [the case's] connection with the pro-Russian group of which I have knowledge and of which Lord Vansittart so clearly and strongly warned me...

Why won't the security outfit [the Security Service] investigate Vansittart's documents on Soviet spies [agents] ... the answer is that Roger Hollis is himself a Soviet agent. And Roger Hollis is backed by the powerful Victor Rothschild who recruited the whole outfit.

Some fifteen years before Chapman Pincher told the world about Hollis, de Courcy was expressing fears that he was the 'Fifth Man' and that Rothschild was the first. Muggeridge's reference to Rothschild and Philby advocating handing over Ultra material direct to the Russians and the fact that the Soviet defector Anatoliy Golitsyn had named Rothschild and his wife Teresa as wartime RIS agents must have been music to de Courcy's ears.[18]

164

What this tale reveals is that there is more to be revealed about Rothschild.

Written by Morris Riley

What the evidence concerning Lord Rothschild, to date, shows is that:

1. Rothschild, unlike Burgess, Maclean, Blunt and Philby was not a Communist, but was intimate with all of the four RIS agents.[19]
2. He had been recruited by Peter Kapitza* to act as an enobler in terms of affecting the above four to become pro-Soviet, the so-called 'original source of evil – the original seducer' i.e. the 'First Man'.
3. During the war he and his wife may have been RIS agents.[20]
4. After the war he changed (or was 'turned') into a mainstream political individual who 'ratted' upon some of his former left-wing associates.

Additionally, it is most interesting how in the mid-1970s, as part of operation CLOCKWORK ORANGE II, the Security Service were willing to 'expose' Rothschild in terms of charging that Edward Heath 'can be shown to be under Soviet control through Lord Rothschild'.[21] This, of course, was pure disinformation and 'black' propaganda.

However, it is striking that the Security Service, years before the rumours floated around about Lord Rothschild, were willing to 'blow' him – be he a Soviet agent, or not. Several years, in fact, before he was publicly linked to Blunt, and now to Philby.

Also of interest, there is a statement by Aharon Moshel, a former Mossad officer, that he was ordered to visit Philby at his Beirut apartment as his arrest by the British was only 'days'

* See reference No. 13

165

away. The Mossad were eager to question him, Philby, about Jewish agents employed by RIS (some of whom they did or did not know about). Could Philby have pointed a finger at Rothschild and his second Jewish wife? This is a historical question, because when questioned, in Moscow, by Phillip Knightley, Philby defended and cleared Rothschild, for whatever a 'defence' and 'clearance' is worth from Philby – after all, when questioned by Nicholas Elliott in December 1962 Philby stated that Blunt was not a Soviet agent and cast totally untrue allegations against the former SIS officer, Tim Milne.

Following the confrontation by Moshel, the Mossad constructed Philby's escape route from the Lebanon: 'After crossing the poorly guarded Syrian border at night in a Lebanese taxi, Philby was received in Damascus by pro-Soviet [henchmen of the leader of the Syrian CP, a Kurd who knew the Kurdish region of northern Syria and Iraq]. They took him through northern Iraq to the village of Dogubazit, where KGB agents whisked him over the Soviet border.'[22]

BOOK REVIEWS

The Philby Files by Genrikh Borovik, ed. Phillip Knightley.
Little, Brown, London, 1944.

The most important point about this book is how from 1934,
when the Russian Intelligence Service (RIS) had Philby working
for it until his death in 1988, they never fully trusted him. This
distrust is encaptured page by page and chapter by chapter, over
three hundred and seventy pages. The RIS did not recruit him as
part of a brilliant, long-term strategy to place Western agents
who would one day hold positions of power, but because it –
mistakenly – believed that his father worked for the British
Secret Intelligence Service (SIS).

As a new recruit Philby was given a 'nice' first assignment –
the distasteful task of spying upon his own father. This he
eagerly did, even though the RIS had actually lied about who he
was really working for. RIS lies and suspicions permeated
decades.

By 1940 their suspicions abounded, and their officer, Elena
Modrzhinskaya, examined Philby's file and those of the other
members of the Cambridge ring in order to decide if they were
genuine Soviet agents or British penetration officers/agents. She
developed a shaky case against Philby. Should Philby have been
a 'plant', therefore then all of the others – Guy Burgess,

Anthony Blunt and John Cairncross – were the same. The RIS London Station, therefore, was informed that the four were in fact SIS agents planted upon Moscow.

The game of deceit and double-dealing continued: the four deceived their colleagues, the SIS, their families and Britain, because of their sincere belief that they were serving the USSR via the RIS as part of a greater cause. As surrogate parents the RIS appeared to trust them totally, but the RIS deceived them because they believed the four to be playing a treble game.

In his Introduction Phillip Knightley writes, 'Borovik draws the startling ... conclusion from this that the main threat to intelligence agents comes not from the counter-intelligence services in the country where they are working, but from their own centre, their own people.' One is not surprised, when the RIS wondered if Philby was a Soviet, British or German agent; and, later presumably a CIA or Mossad agent. How nice to be trusted!

In the book Philby contradicts himself many times. Firstly he reveals his RIS recruiter to have been Maurice Dobb who recruited him during his final term at Cambridge. Pages later he explains: 'It was Edith Tudor-Hart. She brought me into the KGB.' Not much difference indeed.

According to Philby's account, upon his return from Austria she introduced him in London to an RIS officer. Yet, on the other hand, on his way to Austria, when Philby was in Paris he states that he received a letter of recommendation to Paris 'from a lady in Cambridge', and clarified with disarming ease that this 'lady' was actually Dobb. More disinformation. One wonders about the obfuscations.

In a conversation in 1987 with Phillip Knightley in Moscow, Philby claimed that he had learned about Donald Maclean and the RIS 'only after the start of the war', and that he doubted that he (Maclean) had been recruited while at Cambridge. Another lie. He actually recruited Maclean himself, in 1934 at Cambridge.

At one stage the RIS wanted Philby to assassinate General Franco in Spain. He wisely declined. His chances of success were virtually zero, and, had he succeeded he would have been instant dead meat, not an attractive prospect. During the two-year period after Philby had joined SIS, before Russia militarily fought back against Germany, as opposed to wanting to know about German capabilities and intentions, to employ Intelligence terminology, the RIS merely wanted countless biographies from and about Philby to cover the terminological areas of 'Motivation', 'Political', 'Sexual', 'Social' and 'Financial'.

The next most interesting area is what Philby, and Genrikh Borovik via the RIS files, omits, or did not reveal, are suppressed about the career of 'Kim' Philby. Various examples:

(a) The death in 1945 of the RIS officer Konstantin Volkov, a would-be defector to SIS. At London SIS HQ Philby read details of his planned defection, and Philby's denouncement to the RIS caused Volkov to be strapped onto a stretcher and flown from Istanbul to Moscow to meet his execution. His death, according to the former SOE-SIS operative, Colonel 'Billy' Maclean, 'was the worst thing that Philby ever did.'[1]

(b) The recruitment, after the war, of former Nazi war criminals, such as Mikolai Abramtchik, Radislaw Ostrowsky and Stanislaw Stankievich, who were exfiltrated via the 'Rat Line' into the CIA and SIS,[2] thus entering Britain and America.

(c) The infiltration, after the war, of émigré Soviet, CIA/SIS agents into the Soviet Union, who were captured (some were 'turned') imprisoned and/or killed.

(d) Full exposure about the on-going CIS/SIS operations, in the late 1940s and early 1950s into Albania leading to the usual fates of allied agents.

(e) Knew that in the margin of the Albanian débâcle one traitorous British officer, 'C', who during the Albanian operations had been sent to a springboard of the operations, Corfu, at a critical period (his girlfriend worked for Israeli Intelligence, but had been fired when it was discovered that she had Communist affiliations) in the early 1950s discovered the American archaeologist, George McFadden, who had served with the OSS at the end of the war, and subsequently had maintained links with US Intelligence in Cyprus, and was deeply suspicious about 'C'. He suspected that when employed by the Near East Arab Broadcasting Station (NEABS), (SIS-directed and FO funded) 'C' had 'blown' the Albanian operations. No case was ever built up against 'C', who was corrupt and a drunk. McFadden was drowned in mysterious circumstances whilst in the company of 'C'. No inquest was held. 'There was,' to quote a former SIS officer 'a [total] cover-up.' The implication, had it been discovered that an SIS employee had been (CENSORED) would have been most embarrassing, and injurious to SIS-CIA, American relations.[3]

(f) Coupled with George Blake (unpublished) 'shopped' NTS-CIA-SIS operations into the Ukraine in the 1950s,[4] with the usual results.

(g) Provided to the RIS details about worldwide SIS (and CIA) officers and agents. As usual in the USSR they were captured, some 'turned', tortured or killed. Their fates were not any better in parts of the non-Communist world. A major case in point was that of Egypt. As a result of the incompetence of SIS Station Commander, Geoffrey Hinton, Philby learned details about SIS operatives and operations in Egypt; George Blake had assisted in the setting up of the networks. Abdel Nasser and the Egyptian Security Service had details originating from Philby about those SIS activities in Egypt. Twenty arrests then followed, including the Arab News Agency (AND) manager, James Swinburn, Maltese businessman, James Zarb, Marconi Radio employee, Charles Pittuck, and John Thornton Stanley of the Prudential Assurance Company. The Egyptians had learned that Swinburn was running the network whilst in permanent contact with the SIS officer, Oliver Saint John. Swinburn confessed to his role of running the major SIS network, and was executed; several others were given life sentences. Other 'journalists', including Sefton Delmer of the *Daily Express*, Ann Shapley of the *Evening Standard*, and Eileen Travis, an American citizen, working for the *Daily Mail*, were all expelled.

(h) Resulting from contact with CP members in the Middle East, Philby, according to a former CIA officer, gave to the

Russians a steady stream of details about CIA operations, and also the identities of CIA officers/agents. At one point after the CIA had discovered that Philby was betraying American officers and agents, it was decided that he should be 'rubbed out' if the British would not take any action. He was informed that the CIA had a hit team in Beirut to terminate him. There was not, but it was enough to make him clear off.

(i) The inter-relationship in terms of espionage and collaborative activities between Philby and Blake is not covered. Blake had been allowed by SIS to become a so-called 'double' agent, and had been allowed to shop the identities of SIS agents to the RIS. Clearly, the deaths of some of the forty-two agents he was imprisoned for can be laid at the doors of SIS.

(j) Philby claims that he was not aware of any CIA or SIS surveillance whilst in the Middle East. For an old professional like 'Kim' not so, the serving CIA officers, Miles Copeland, Kermit Roosevelt and Wilbur Crane Eveland did so; James Russell Barracks masterminded the CIA surveillance on Philby. On the British side, he had been observed by F. W. D. Deakin, and the SIS-employed journalist Arthur Cooke. Mossad officer Aharon Moshel also had an investigative role.

(k) Back in the USSR, in 1971, Philby was appointed head of the Department of Western Propaganda for the semi-official Novosti news agency, and in an article in *Kudumaa*, he identified many real or alleged SIS agents, as he also did in *Izvestia*. Some of the allegations rebounded when three of the alleged agents brought libel suits against Tass, and were awarded damages of £6,250 each. This débâcle is not covered in Borovik's book.

Of interest to Philby watchers is the re-emergence of the journalist, Patrick Seale. In *The Philby Files*, it is claimed that Philby allegedly recruited Seale for SIS, and, according to the publisher's editorial director Anthony Samson, Seale had issued a writ against Little, Brown over this matter.[5] In a letter from Samson to an author of one of the Philby books, he thanks him for the most useful information about Seale. This author had been informed by a former SIS officer (CENSORED).

Lastly, there are the accounts of how Philby fled from Beirut in January 1963. According to Philby, he exited by a Soviet ship, the *Dolmatova*, all the way to Odessa. On the other hand, according to the Mossad officer, Aharon Moshel, the Mossad discovered his route as being overland via Syria, at one point in the hands of a Kurdish CP henchman, into Turkey and back into the USSR.[6] Somebody was lying. But who?

In all, this is a most interesting book and does not overlap with any of the other books about Philby. What is of most interest, in addition to what it reveals, is what it does not reveal – in one word: suppresses. One newspaper article, in the *Sunday Express* of 5 June 1988, postulated as to the threats the book would contain. In the event of publication, it did not.

Treason In The Blood by Anthony Cave Brown. Robert Hale, London, 1995.

This book is too long, over 600 pages, and too boring, even for Philby specialists, even though it received an excellent review in America.[7] Examined are Philby Senior, the famed Arabist, and far more examined is Philby Junior, the notorious Secret Intelligence Service (SIS) officer, RIS officer, CIA and sometime a Mossad agent. Brown has read all of the books and articles about 'Kim' Philby, had interviews in America, Britain and Russia (not all of his sources are revealed) in addition to checking various archives. All this material is turgidly regurgitated in a book which could easily have edited down to 300 or even 200 pages; and still easily have made its main points – not that there are many, one may add.

Another new Russian Intelligence Service (RIS) recruiter of Philby is brought forward in terms of being Arnold Deutsch upon Philby's return from Austria in 1934. As in the case of nearly all the other books about Philby[8] his time in the Middle East is not adequately covered. There is no mention of the operations he was involved in for the CIA, SIS, RIS and the Mossad. Unlike as covered in Tom Bower's excellent *The Perfect English Spy*, about Sir Dick White, nothing is mentioned about SIS incompetence and corruption[9] or CIA disinformation about Philby. In fact, Brown's book has been written so as not to offend the CIA, SIS or RIS. No mention is made about how Philby recruited ex-Nazi war criminals for the CIA-SIS; caused the deaths of CIA-SIS agents in Russia, Albania and the Middle East. The names of the two SIS officers who re-recruited and reassigned Philby for SIS work in Beirut, the Chief, Sir John Sinclair, and his Vice-Chief, George Kennedy Young (via a post they arranged with the proprietor of the *Observer*, David Astor, who was told of Philby's SIS role) are not revealed in this role. The only new information about the Middle East is about an aborted plan by SIS to assassinate Egypt's President Abdel Nasser; nothing is mentioned of Young's parallel plan which included Special Air Service (SAS) involvement.

Considering what has been published about Philby's time, 1963–88, in Russia Brown's book does not contain much, or indeed anything, new. The two Russian chapters are notable for glaring omissions: Philby's 'drying-out' in Kuibishev upon his defection in 1963; constant RIS distrust; his naming SIS officers/agents in 1971[10]; and other activities as described in books published about Philby.

Brown's biggest goolie: p. 595, 'Blake had escaped from Wormwood Scrubs prison with the help of the IRA...' Sean Bourke would rotate in his grave if he could hear this.

Verdict: do not bother or waste your money, £25.00, on this book. Instead, buy or borrow Tom Bowyer's book, or buy Morris Riley's book now illegally selling for £35.00.[11] *Treason In The Blood* is an inadequate and most disappointing book.

My Five Cambridge Friends by Yuri Modin. Headline, London, 1994.

This is an excellent book. Unlike Borovik, Modin was an actual RIS case officer, and it shows in terms of experience and knowledge. He nails down the recruitment of Philby:

For over thirty years now, journalists, writers and self-proclaimed experts have speculated about how Philby was originally recruited. A dense fog of disinformation cloaks the entire episode. At least five men, over the years, have claimed that it was they who found the spy of the century. I myself have read reports by several different intelligence officers who swore that they alone had accomplished the exploit. This is any intelligence officer's dream, of course. But it was all nonsense. I don't want to sound pretentious, but each time I could tell they were lying. The times, places and individuals they cited were hopelessly mixed up.

He goes on to explain that Philby was not recruited whilst in Austria. Upon his return to London his wife, Litzi, made contacts with the local Communists, notably Edith Tudor-Hart. She in turn, after the RIS had made their usual checks, brought Philby into contact with Arnold Deutsch, an NKVD illegal operative. So much for Maurice Dobb.

Modin also contradicts Borovik when he states that it was Philby himself who proposed to the RIS that he should personally assassinate Franco; and he also provides details about the operations, most of them, he was involved in, and the arrests and deaths therein caused by Philby.

As in the case of other books about RIS officers, it starts out by describing how Modin was recruited and his training in Russia. It really gets into its stride when he is posted to London in 1948. He totally describes his dealings with the Cambridge Five in terms of their good points, warts and all; how they totally ran rings around the 'professional' Security Service watchers (let us not forget that between 1945 and 1990 the Service on their own never captured one foreign agent). His description of the Burgess-Maclean defection in 1951 is quite suspenseful. Lastly, he covers how Philby and co. dealt with, or could not deal with the pressures of their double lives: Philby and Blunt were able to, not so Burgess and Maclean.

Verdict: read this book, you will not be disappointed.

SECURITY SERVICE (MI5) INPUT

Enough has already been written about SIS. Let us see how the Security Service[1] received, perceived and responded to this book.

When in January 1991 discussing the recently-shown spy film on BBC TV, *The Whistleblower*, in which the star Michael Caine discovered that his son, working for GCHQ, had been murdered under instructions from the Security Service, a currently serving officer observed to the author: 'It does happen. Another department deals with it. I can't say who.' It was a most interesting conversation with a security officer (a copy of the book had been given to him) who had obviously been authorized to disclose the information to me but who cannot be named here. The confirmation was not surprising. After all, such terminations are merely sanctioned by the Security Service; the serving officers would not dirty their own hands. It is always sub-contracted to private security firms, former members of the SAS, ex-soldiers and others. (The reader is referred to pages 149–50.)

Twenty-five years ago SIS was the major intelligence organization in Northern Ireland. It employed agents. One such agent was Major Fred Holroyd. He had been recruited by the SIS officer, Craig Smellie, for whom he had a very high regard. In the words of Holroyd ('Five' is military intelligence terminology for MI5):

> In 1975–76 Northern Ireland became one of the battlegrounds for a damaging feud between SIS and the Security Service. ['Five' wanted to take over from SIS.] When Five took over, people like myself, steady regimental officers with a sense of right and wrong, were replaced by these Five characters who were out for everything they could get. They were quite ruthless about exposing their sources to risks. The decent people were replaced by very ambitious, mean, nasty people.[2]

The changeover had one immediate consequence. Instead of meeting Smellie (before being illegally yanked out of Ireland) Holroyd met with the new man of the Security Service:

> As I left the meeting I was grabbed by Keith Farnes, SAS, the G2 Intelligence of Army HQ, who pulled me into a doorway and told me that one of our IRA deep cover agents had been discovered by the IRA, thanks to Five tipping them off – all within the week that the information had been handed over to Five. The handler, a Staff Sergeant whom I knew, had gone into an Army bunker and shot himself. He could not live with himself and what Five had done.[3]

As part of getting rid of SIS agents, Holroyd was caught in the crossfire. He was falsely taken to the military mental hospital, Netley in Hampshire and incarcerated therein. Subsequently after being expelled from the Army, Holroyd enlisted in the Rhodesian SAS. He lived, but other former military officers who had acted as SIS agents in Northern Ireland, did not. SIS suspects that their murders had been sanctioned by the Security Service as a result of the fall-out in Northern Ireland.

One would have thought that the Security Service would have wanted to hang on to the Northern Ireland SIS military agents for essential intelligence. But no, they did not. Instead they wanted to give the message that 'We are in charge now. Forget Six [MI6]. We are ruthless bastards.'

176

When the Security Service or any other Service take a decision at a very high level to kill an intelligence target, such an operation includes the plans of:

1. A surveillance to confirm the target's daily movements and personal life-style;
2. The address of the said target for access and the best time and location for the 'wet job' re the target;
3. The destination of the victim and method of disposal has to be decided in terms of: an 'accident' or 'death' by natural causes.

Should one expect these pages to raise questions, or even an enquiry in the House of Commons, forget it. The PM, his Ministers and MPs on both sides of the House are scared of the Security Service. The reason is that the Service have got the 'dirt', actual and manufactured, on them. Let us not forget that one of the best ways for a Service officer to gain promotion is to obtain the dirt on a politician, under the categories of 'political', 'social', 'sexual' and 'financial'. One only has to look into the cases of Harold Wilson (code-named OATSHEAF), Tony Benn, Edward Heath and Leon Brittan, who were all unjustly and incorrectly smeared by Five.

Morris Riley, January 1999

NOTES AND REFERENCES

1 The New Recruit
1 Kim Philby, *My Silent War*, MacGibbon & Kee, London, 1968, p. 1.
2 ibid., p. 2.
3 Patrick Seale and Maureen McConville, *Philby, the Long Road to Moscow*, Hamish Hamilton, London, 1973, p. 118.
4 Bruce Page, David Leitch and Phillip Knightley, *Philby, the Spy Who Betrayed a Generation*, Sphere, London, 1980, p. 132.
5 E. H. Cookridge, *The Third Man*, Barker, London, 1968, p. 95.
6 Andrew Boyle, *The Climate of Treason*, Coronet, London, 1980, p. 203.
7 id., No. 1, p. 3.
8 Bickham Sweet-Escott, *Baker Street Irregular*, Methuen, London, 1965, p. 17.
9 id., No. 5, p. 98.
10 ibid., pp. 99–100.
11 J. R. M. Butler, *Grand Strategy*, Vol. II, HMSO, London, 1957.
12 Hugh Dalton, *The Fateful Years: Memoirs 1931–1945*, Muller, London, 1957, p. 378.
13 id., No. 1, p. 16.
14 id., No. 3, p. 129.
15 ibid., p. 134.
16 A personal communication from the late Colonel Vivian to the authors Patrick Seale and Maureen McConville. id., No. 3, p. 135.
17 Hugh Trevor-Roper, *The Philby Affair*, William Kimber, London, 1968, p. 27.

2 The Coming Messiah

1 Kim Philby, *My Silent War*, MacGibbon & Kee, London, 1968, pp. 31–32.

2 Bruce Page, David Leitch and Phillip Knightley, *Philby, the Spy Who Betrayed a Generation*, Sphere, London, 1980, p. 172.

3 Augustin Souchy Bauer, *With the Peasants of Aragon*, Cienfuegos Press, Orkney, 1982, p. 8.

4 ibid., pp. 11–12.

5 Miguel Garcia, *Franco's Prisoner*, Rupert Hart-Davis, London, 1972, p. 28.

6 Albert Meltzer, *A New World in Our Hearts*, Cienfuegos Press, Orkney, 1979, p. 48.

7 Miguel Garcia, op. cit., p. 28.

8 E. H. Cookridge, *The Third Man*, Barker, London, 1968, p. 107.

9 ibid., p. 108.

10 id., No. 1, pp. 44–5.

11 Chapman Pincher, *Their Trade is Treachery*, Sidgwick and Jackson, London, 1982, p. 269.

12 id., No. 1, p. 52.

13 ibid., p. 68.

14 op. cit., p. 72.

15 op. cit., p. 75.

16 id., No. 8, p. 140.

17 Quoted by Page, Leitch and Knightley, pp. 190–91.

18 ibid., p. 191.

19 Chapman Pincher in *Their Trade is Treachery*, p. 38.

20 ibid., pp. 38–39.

21 id., No. 2, p. 200.

22 Quoted from a letter from Malcolm Muggeridge to Andrew Boyle.

23 *Sunday Telegraph*, 12 March, 1978.

24 Even as late as 1982, Greene was still in correspondence with Philby. In fact, letters from Philby to Greene postmarked Cuba, in early 1982, gave rise to an article suggesting that Philby had popped up in Cuba and was advising President Castro. *Daily Express*, 5 May 1982.

25 id., No. 1, p. 97.

3 Enter George Blake

1 E. H. Cookridge, *Shadow of a Spy*, Leslie Frewin Publishers Ltd, London, 1967, p. 26.

2 ibid., p. 36.
3 Andrew Boyle, *The Climate of Treason*, Coronet, London, 1980, p. 349.
4 id., No. 1, p. 73.
5 ibid., p. 79.
6 op. cit., p. 80.
7 id., No. 3, p. 349.
8 Kim Philby, *My Silent War*, MacGibbon & Kee, London, 1968, p. 102.
9 ibid., p. 100.
10 id., No. 11, p. 145.
11 Anthony Verrier, *Through the Looking Glass*, Jonathan Cape, London, 1983, p. 59.
12 id., No. 8, p. 109.

4 The Merchant of Death
1 Bruce Page, David Leitch and Phillip Knightley, *Philby, the Spy Who Betrayed a Generation*, Sphere, London, 1980, p. 210.
2 Patrick Seale and Maureen McConville, *Philby, the Long Road to Moscow*, Hamish Hamilton, London, 1973, p. 200.
3 id., No. 1, p. 211.
4 ibid., quoted by the authors.
5 Harry Rositzke, *The KGB*, Sidgwick & Jackson, London, 1983, p. 152.
6 ibid.
7 *Daily Telegraph*, March 29 1983.
8 ibid., November 3 1981.
9 Letter from C. M. Woodhouse to the author.
10 id., No. 5, p. 151.
11 id., No. 7.
12 Information from Commander Courtney to the author.
13 John Luftus, *The Belarus Secret*, Penguin Books, London, 1983, p. 168.
14 Interview on *Panorama*, BBC TV, 4 July, 1983.
15 id., No. 13, p. 16.
16 ibid., p. 25.
17 Report by Sgt Soennecken, *Congressional Record Appendix*, 7 August 1948, Nuremburg Document No. 3047, p. 5.
18 id., No. 13, p. 34.
19 op. cit., p. 197.

20 Barbie in 1945 moved into a British zone in Germany. He was first
   and foremost an SIS agent, loaned by SIS to DAD, followed by the
   CIC.
21 Kim Philby, *My Silent War*, MacGibbon & Kee, London 1968, p.
   116.
22 id., No. 1, p. 122.
23 ibid., p. 165.
24 State Department document, quoted in 'The 1950 "invasion" of
   Albania' by Bill Bland, The Albanian Society, Ilford, 1984, p. 4.
25 id., No. 21, p. 117.
26 Anthony Verrier, *Through the Looking Glass*, Jonathan Cape,
   London, 1983, p. 72.
27 Christopher Felix,* *A Short Course in the Secret War*, New York,
   1963, pp. 55–56.
28 David Smiley, *Albanian Assignment*, Sphere Books, London, 1985,
   p. 164.
29 Phillip Knightley, 'The Man Who Was Q', (date unknown) *Sunday
   Times Magazine Supplement*.
30 ibid.
31 op. cit.
32 id., No. 21, p. 119.
33 Roger Faligot, *Les Services Speciaux de Sa Majesté*, Temps Actuals,
   Paris, 1982.
34 ibid.
35 id., No. 1, p. 215.
36 Transcript from a BBC TV programme, 30 September 1984.
37 <u>NEABS, Limassol, Cyprus.</u>
38 Private source.

5 The Ukraine

1 Bruce Page, David Leitch and Phillip Knightley, *Philby, the Spy Who
  Betrayed a Generation*, Sphere Books, London, 1980, pp. 216–217.
2 ibid., p. 217.
3 ibid.
4 ibid., p. 218.
5 Kim Philby, *My Silent War*, MacGibbon & Kee, London, 1968, p. 120.
6 *NTS – Introduction to a Russian Freedom Party*, NTS
  Publication, West Germany. (Undated) p. 4.

* A pseudonym used by the former CIA officer James McCargar.

181

7 Louis Hagen, *The Secret War for Europe*, Macdonald, London, 1968, p. 164.

8 ibid.

9 ibid.

10 ibid., p. 165.

11 id., No. 5, p. 120.

12 id., No. 1, p. 218.

13 id., No. 5, p. 120.

14 id., No. 1, p. 219.

15 id., No. 5, p. 120.

16 ibid., p. 121.

17 ibid., p. 220.

18 Geoffrey Stewart-Smith, *The Defeat of Communism*, Ludgate Press, London, 1964, p. 336.

19 Roger Faligot, *Les Services Speciaux de Sa Majesté*, Temps Actuals, Paris, 1982.

20 Information to the author from George Miller, chief NTS representative in Britain.

21 Information from a confidential source, who knew Blake. Blake totally confided in this source.

22 E. H. Cookridge, *Shadow of a Spy*, Leslie Frewin Publishers Ltd, London, 1967, p. 95.

23 ibid., p. 103.

6 A Downfall – and Iran

1 E. H. Cookridge, *The Third Man*, Arthur Barker, London, 1968, p. 235.

2 ibid., p. 236.

3 Leonard Mosley, *Power Play*, Weidenfeld & Nicolson, London, 1973, p. 16.

4 Fred Halliday, *Arabia Without Sultans*, Pelican Books, London, 1974, p. 472.

5 Montague Woodhouse, *Something Ventured*, Granada, London, 1982, p. 105.

6 id., No. 3, p. 165.

7 *Observer*, 26 May 1985, p. 10.

8 id., No. 5.

9 Kermit Roosevelt, *Countercoup*, McGraw-Hill Book Company, USA, 1st edition, 1979, p. 107. The first edition was published in late 1979, but within a matter of days, McGraw-Hill withdrew the entire edition

after strenuous protests by the British Petroleum Company (BP) over the identification of its predecessor, Anglo-Iranian Oil Company, as the originator of the plan to overthrow Mossadeq. They were quite correct; after all, the coup had been instigated by the SIS and CIA. Roosevelt had wanted to disguise the identity of the original instigators – perhaps as a result of advice from British and American intelligence.

10 *New Statesman*, 29 May 1981, p. 8.
11 *Guardian*, 28 July 1980.
12 id., No. 5, p. 124.
13 ibid., p. 125.
14 id., No. 3, p. 172.
15 *Countercoup* book review by Neville George, CAIB, Washington, No. 7, December 1979–80, p. 29.
16 See 'British Spies Meddle in Middle East Affairs': Hirbernia, Dublin, 3 March 1980.
17 id., No. 9, p. 108.
18 ibid.
19 Andrew Weir, Jonathan Bloch and Pat Fitzgerald, 'Sun sets over the other Empire': *The Middle East*, London, October 1981, p. 39.
20 id., No. 3, p. 175.
21 ibid., p. 175.
22 id., No. 19.
23 Philip Agee and Louis Wolf, *Dirty Work*, Lyle Stuart Inc., USA, 1978, p. 672.
24 *Counterspy*, Washington, Vol. 4, No. 4, September–October, 1980, p. 3.
25 id., No. 3, p. 176.
26 id., No. 4, p. 473.
27 *Saturday Evening Post*, 6 November 1954.

7 The Middle East

1 *The New Leader*, New York, 25 June 1984.
2 ibid.
3 An article in the 23 April 1950 issue, *Sunday Mail*, Nicosia.
4 Private source.
5 By 355 votes to 61.

8 The Spy Who Returned From the Cold

1 Andrew Boyle, *The Climate of Treason*, Coronet, London, 1980, p. 449.

2 'A Lost Correspondent', *The Economist*, 6 July 1963, p. 21.
3 ibid.
4 id., No. 1, p. 450.
5 John Fisher, *Burgess & Maclean*, London, 1977, p. 207.
6 Patrick Seale and Maureen McConville, *Philby, the Long Road to Moscow*, Hamish Hamilton, London 1973, p. 240.
7 ibid., p. 237.
8 E. H. Cookridge, *The Third Man*, Barker, London, 1968, p. 234.
9 E. H. Cookridge, *Shadow of a Spy*, Barker, London, 1968, p. 182.
10 Bruce Page, David Leitch and Phillip Knightley, *Philby, the Spy Who Betrayed a Generation*, Sphere Books, London, 1980, p. 144.
11 ibid.
12 Andrew Weir, Jonathan Bloch, Patrick Fitzgerald, 'Sun Sets Over the other Empire', *The Middle East*, London, October, 1981, p. 40.
13 Wilbur Crane Eveland, *Ropes of Sand*, W. W. Norton, New York, 1980, p. 170.
14 ibid.
15 Chapman Pincher, *Their Trade is Treachery*, Sidgwick and Jackson, London, 1982, p. 206.
16 Chapman Pincher, *Inside Story*, Sidgwick and Jackson, London, 1978, p. 9.
17 *Observer*, 12 May 1957.
18 id., No. 15.
19 ibid.
20 id., No. 10, p. 285.
21 ibid.
22 ibid.
23 Ray Alan, *The Beirut Pipeline*, Farra Straus, New York and Collins, London, 1980, p. 18.
24 id., No. 10, p. 289.
25 J. Bloch and P. Fitzgerald, *British Intelligence and Covert Action*, Junction Books, London, 1983, p. 122.
26 id., No. 13, p. 169.
27 ibid., p. 235.

9 Lebanese Capers
1 Bruce Page, David Leitch and Phillip Knightley, *Philby, the Spy Who Betrayed a Generation*, Sphere Books, London, 1980, p. 310.
2 Wilbur Crane Eveland, *Ropes of Sand*, W. W. Norton, New York, 1980, p. 251.

3 ibid., p. 252.
4 ibid., p. 291.
5 Sir Humphrey Trevelyan, *The Middle East in Revolution*, Macmillan, London, 1970, pp. 135–6.
6 id., No. 2, p. 274.
7 ibid., p. 274 & 300.
8 Information to the author from Wilbur Crane Eveland.
9 id., No. 1, p. 314.
10 'Lebanon Landing', *The Economist*, 19 July 1958, p. 206.
11 ibid., 'The Balance Sheet of Intervention', p. 183.
12 Sir Anthony Nutting, *The Arabs*, Mentor Books, New York, 1964, p. 346.
13 British armed intervention ended any possible revolutionary upsurge in Jordan.
14 Hanna Batatu, *The Old Social Classes and the Revolutionary Movements of Iraq*, Princeton University Press, 1978, p. 803.

10 NorthYemen

1 Fred Halliday, *Arabia Without Sultans*, Pelican Books, London, 1979, p. 81.
2 The imams of the Yemen trace their descent from the Prophet's son-in-law Ali.
3 Taxation was ferocious; the minimal rate was 10 per cent for all crops, but the tax collector was able to extract furthes sums fixed at will. Crops were measured on sight leading to very imprecise estimates. The peasants had to bribe the tax collector in order to stop him from taking even more in tax. Animals were also taxed at a fixed rate per head.
4 Dana Adams Schmidt, *Yemen, The Unknown War*, Bodley Head, London, 1968, p. 41.
5 Colonel Edgar O'Ballance, *The War in the Yemen*, Faber, London, 1971, p. 53.
6 Information to the author from a Colonel who knew al-Badr.
7 Patrick Seale and Maureen McConville, *Philby, the Long Road to Moscow*, Hamish Hamilton, London, 1973, p. 257.
8 *The Economist*, 27 October 1962, p. 336.
9 Julian Amery, (son-in-law of Prime Minister Macmillan), as chairman at a lecture given at the RUSI called 'The War in the Yemen' by Colonel Neil McLean, 20 October 1965.
10 Information from Julian Amery to the author.

185

11 id., No. 9.
12 Information from Colonel David Stirling (the founder of the SAS) to the author.
13 Information from Colonel McLean to the author.
14 ibid.
15 ibid.
16 id., No. 10.
17 id., No. 9.
18 For details of Colonel McLean's work for SIS, see 'Ex-spies I've known in the Commons', Andrew Roth, *New Statesman*, 28 November 1986, p. 14.
19 id., No. 10.
20 Tony Geraghty, *Who Dares Wins*, Fontana, London, 1981, p. 112.
21 *The Investigative Researcher's Handbook*, Refract, London, 1983, p. 123.
22 Information from Colonel James Johnson to the author.
23 *Daily Telegraph*, 4 February 1970.
24 id., No. 4, p. 161.
25 *Time Out*, 28 July 1978.
26 Colonel David Smiley, *Arabian Assignment*, Leo Cooper, London, 1975, p. 156.
27 id., No. 22.
28 id., No. 12.
29 id., No. 22.
30 ibid.
31 'The Pedigree Dogs of War', *Time Out*, London, July 1977, p. 10.
32 *Time Out*, 28 July 1978.
33 id., No. 22.
34 Information to the author from Mr J. Adams, Foreign Manager, *Sunday Times*, January 1983.
35 id., No. 22.
36 Letter to the author from Colonel Smiley, dated July 1983.
37 id., No. 12.
38 id., No. 13.
39 Kim Philby, *My Silent War*, MacGibbon & Kee, London 1968, p. 152.
40 ibid., p. 153.
41 op. cit.
42 op. cit.
43 Whilst in London, it is alleged that he associated with John Vassall,

the homosexual Admiralty spy. Vassall was part of an RIS-organized homosexual circle. He also dined with two MPs in the House of Commons, who also made frequent visits to his flat in Dolphin Square. Both MPs were from the Conservative Party. One was later elevated to the House of Lords. Vassall claimed that the MP now in the Lords, slept with him at his flat and that both took him out separately on numerous occasions. Although acquaintances, each was curious to discover from Vassall the other's homosexual tendencies. One of the two had been befriended by a Communist diplomat, who took him to social events. Vassall believed that both men were open to bribery or blackmail by foreign Security Services as a result of their activities which he described as on the fringe of the twilight world; the British Security Service also believed the same. Because of their belief, they had a homosexual agent infiltrate the RIS-organized group. The agent was spotted, and was discovered dead, throttled with a towel.

44 Information from a confidential source to the author.
45 ibid.
46 Private source.
47 ibid.
48 James Rusbridger, *The Intelligence Game*, The Bodley Head, London, 1989, p. 53.

11 Back in the USSR

1 'Communist Bloc Intelligence Activities in the United States'. Hearing before the sub-committee to investigate the administration of the Internal Security Act and other Internal Security Laws of the Committee on the Judiciary United States Senate, Ninety-Fourth Congress. Second Session. Part 2. 12 April 1976, pp. 74–5.
2 During late 1983, the Soviet Union took great exception to President Reagan ordering the US Marines into the Lebanon. Something had to be done, and it was. Suicide bombers attacked the Marine base in Beirut and caused the deaths of numerous Marines. This incident acted as a major factor in the subsequent withdrawal of US troops from Lebanon.
     'Two weeks before explosive-packed trucks crashed into the American and French barracks, Israeli Intelligence Services warned that something was brewing, but the report went unheeded. As French intelligence have reconstructed the affair, US agents watching Damascus airport photographed two men who descended from a

Soviet plane on Saturday, October 15, and were whisked away in a black limousine with a military escort. Three other cars loaded with KGB agents and members of the Syrian secret police run by Rifaat el-Assad, the President's brother, followed. Their destination was one of the principle terrorist-training camps of the Middle East, run by Syrians but used as a shelter for the Palestine organisation, Saika, and fanatics selected from Lebanon's 1.2 million Shia Moslems. The camp was on the outskirts of Damascus. Identifying the VIPs took time, and the co-operating services could hardly believe their own specialists when they were informed that the new arrivals were high explosive specialists from the Darjavna Sigournost, the Bulgarian secret service.' (H du B Reports, Vol XXVI, October 1983, Monte Carlo.)

The departure of US troops in February 1984, was described by Soviet officials to Lebanese reporters as 'a victory for Moscow'.

Now the USSR made their moves. Some of the 9,000 Russian advisers and troops in Syria moved into the Beka valley in Lebanon which was subjected then to heavy Israeli artillery fire. Evidence which came to light in 1984 suggested that the Soviet Union was preparing to move directly into Lebanon themselves, having the immediate goal of taking over from the US the task of building up an effective Lebanese army by supplying arms and military personnel. Initial Soviet involvement came through the Druze militias and their commander, Walid Jumblatt's military chief, Anwar el Fatiri. He carries the rank of Colonel in the Syrian army, received after graduation from the Soviet army's staff college in Moscow. One security report described Fatiri as a Marxist 'who usually follows the Moscow line without question'. Via el Fatiri, the Syrians and Russians could reach the Druzes behind Jumblatt's back.

Early in December 1983, the Soviet Union sent weapons and cash to Lebanon for el Fatiri to hand over to the Druze militia chiefs loosely allied under Jumblatt. Consequently, the chiefs were won over. Next Fatiri persuaded the Druze leadership to force Jumblatt to go to Moscow and personally negotiate with the Russians. Nahib Berri, the Minister for Southern Lebanon affairs and reconstruction, and the go-between regarding a 1985 airline hijacking in Beirut soon followed. Awaiting the Lebanese Prime Minister, Rashid Karameh, in Moscow was a draft agreement about Soviet arms supplies for Lebanon, complete with Soviet instructors, to rebuild the Lebanese army, from the bottom upwards.

188

3 An award established in 1972 and given mainly to foreigners who have performed particularly valuable services to the Soviet Union.

4 Certain Western politicians, including Mrs Thatcher, thought that the introduction of such missiles would add to the West's deterrent and would enable them to 'bargain from strength' and beat the Russians into making concessions. Not understanding the Russian mind, Western politicians were somewhat surprised that the Russians did not cave in, but themselves introduced new missiles in order to gain mutuality.

5 The WPC has an interesting history. It dates from August of 1948 when it was initiated in Poland. It was actually founded in 1949 in Paris under the name of the World Committee of Partisans for Peace; its present title was adopted in 1950. In 1951 the French government on the grounds of 'fifth column activities' expelled the WPC from France. Next they moved to Prague in Czechoslovakia and moved again in 1954 to Vienna. Operating at first as the World Council of Peace, they were once again banned for 'activities directed against the Austrian state'. However, the organization continued to operate in Vienna as the International Institute for Peace (IIP) until September 1968 when the WPC transferred its HQ to Helsinki. The IIP secretariat remained in Vienna, while the WPC had its information office in East Berlin.

President of the WPC was Romesh Chandra, a prominent Indian Communist, who has held the position since 1977. He was pro-Soviet. When the question of the treatment of USSR and Czechoslovakian dissidents was raised by the War Registers' International at the World Congress of Peace Forces in Moscow in 1973, Chandra stated that any peace groups which adopted an anti-Soviet stance 'ceased to be genuine peace organizations'. Two years later in Moscow, he openly announced that the WPC 'reacts positively to all Soviet initiatives in international affairs'. The then Soviet Union, as one would expect, was effusive in its praise of the WPC and President Chandra. At a Kremlin ceremony in June 1981, the USSR President, Leonid Brezhnev, presented Chandra with the prestigious Order of Lenin and cited his service to the 'ideals of peace, his ceaselessness in the bitter struggle against the forces of militarism and aggression'. These glowing attributions did not assist Chandra when, in 1980, he wanted to visit Britain. He found himself detained at Heathrow airport and then put on a flight to Warsaw after being refused permission to enter the UK by Home Secretary, Willie Whitelaw, on the grounds of his organization being 'a disguised instrument of Soviet foreign policy'. (Chandra had been due to attend a weekend meeting organized by the All Britain Peace Liaison Group.* Other speakers due to attend were Terence Parry, TUC President and fireman's leader; Arthur Scargill, then the Yorkshire miners' leader; Jo Richardson, then Labour MP for Barking.) In Parliament, Mr James Lamond** a Labour MP, protested about the Home Secretary's action and added that the aim of the meeting was to try and step up peace activities in Britain through the trade union movement, thus paraphrasing the strategy outlined in the Moscow-published *Communist* journal of September 1983.

The WPC has not only been described as a Soviet Front organization by the British government: Stanislav Leuchenko, a former KGB Major, told the US House of Representatives Select Committee on Intelligence, in Washington in July 1982, that his assignment was to work with the Soviet Peace Committee to manipulate the WPC which he described as 'one of the major Soviet Front organizations'. Additionally, defector Igor Glagolev added further details when questioned by reporter John Rees:

Q. You were an official of the World Peace Council [WPC] an organisa- tion which works with a number of US groups ranging from the Communist Party, USA, through the disarmament coalition, the coalition for a new Foreign and Military Policy, to the disarmament and anti- nuclear power Mobilisation for Survival. What can you tell us of this operation?
A. I know this programme very well. The World Peace Council is an organization which is officially considered inter-nation and non-political, but is actually subordinated to both the International Departments of the CPSU Central Committee and to the KGB. The aim of the World Peace Council is to influence masses of people in the democratic countries. The International Department of the Central Committee, CPSU, chooses members or prospective members of the World Peace Council. It actually appoints them, both the Soviet citizens and the citizens of the foreign countries. There is a special fund the Central Committee uses [provided by the Soviet Peace Committee]. The money is collected by the churches in the Soviet Union and the believers think this money will be used for a real peace movement.

* The 1980 chairman was Gordon Shaffer, also a Vice-President of the WPC.
** President of the British Peace Assembly, Vice-President of the British Soviet Friendship Society, and also the WPC.

Ruth Tosek, a former senior interpreter at several Moscow-controlled organizations, further confirmed the sources of WPC funds from the Soviet bloc in a letter published by the *New Statesman*, 17 October 1980:

> All funds of these organisations, in local and in hard currency, are provided above all by the Soviet Union, but also by other East European Satellite countries on the basis of set contribution rates, paid by the governments of these countries through various channels.

She also confirmed the degree of Soviet direction:

> In addition to clandestine Soviet financing of the World Peace Council, its leaders and propaganda are directed by the International Department of the Soviet Communist Party's Committee. The WPC is usually the first of the various fronts to promote new propaganda initiatives from Moscow, and co-ordinate the activities of several other Communist front groups.
>
> Through direct lines to key WPC officials, the USSR is able to influence final decisions on WPC projects and activities, and the content of communiques, resolutions and statements issued at council events.
>
> On the financial side, the English language weekly *Moscow News*, No. 19, 1981, stated that the Soviet Peace fund financed some of the WPC's 'large public initiatives'. Money collected by the Soviet Peace Fund is channelled to the WPC HQ in Helsinki either through the International Department or through the SCDP. Many peace committee chapters, (affiliated with the WPC) receive Soviet assistance via the local Embassies and Communist parties. The CIA has estimated that the WPC receives £25 million – or more – a year from the Kremlin.

In an angry interview, WPC's President, Chandra, said that the State Department in Washington was 'spreading lies' by suggesting that he was fronting for Moscow and receiving £25 million a year in Kremlin money, filtered to his Helsinki base through the KGB's active section. 'It's a lie,' he added. However, owing to financial irregularities, the WPC was forced to withdraw its application for recalcitration to Category I Consultative Status in its relationship with the UN Economic and Social Council (ECOSOC) at a session of the Committee on Non-Government Organizations held between 9–19 February 1981, in New York. According to the ECOSOC Report (16 March 1981) WPC accounts 'are not submitted to independent audit ... the financial statements submitted to the

191

committee covered only a fraction of WPC's actual income and expenditure. In its application, the WPC also stated that it does not receive contributions from any government ... but the representative of the organization [Romesh Chandra] carefully avoided answering specific questions put to him by members of the committee on that point. It is clear, however, that the WPC has received large-scale financial support from [Communist] government sources, and has gone to great lengths to conceal the fact from the committee.'

12 The Philby Jigsaw

1 'Special Office Brief', 14 November 1985.

2 39 out of 70 pages of a booklet entitled *Russia's Enemies in Britain* (by Reginald Bishop, editor of the *Russian Today Society*) were devoted to attacking de Courcy.

3 Churchill told the story to an Allied head of state after the war.

4 De Courcy was prosecuted. Initially, he was to have been prosecuted on a charge of receiving too much money (over and above a minimum subscription figure) and pocketing the balance. Bank statements held by de Courcy proved otherwise. However, he was charged for not receiving enough money, when Chairman of a Purchasing Trust. During the trial, his defence discovered that essential documents were missing – de Courcy could not prove his innocence, and he was jailed. Whilst in jail his counsel obtained statements from 20 witnesses, thus proving his case. He appeared before the Chancery Division in July 1968, and was awarded £6,000 costs and all other claims against him 'released and extinguished'. De Courcy left court satisfied. Both he and his prison escorts expected him to be released from prison. He was not; and had to serve until 1969. Upon his release, he again tried to re-open his case. The Home Secretary was petitioned – no result.

He tried to sue the Home Secretary – this was held to be *ultra vires*. He tried the European Commission of Human Rights – once again held to be *ultra vires*. He is still pursuing his case.

5 Donald Southerland, *The Fourth Man*, Secker and Warburg, London, 1980, p. 53.

6 Michael Straight, *After Long Silence*, Collins, London, 1983, pp. 94–5.

7 Bruce Page, David Leitch and Phillip Knightley, *Philby, the Spy Who Betrayed a Generation*, Sphere, London, 1980, p. 92.

8 Andrew Boyle, *The Climate of Treason*, Coronet, London, 1980, p. 233.

9   ibid., p. 221.

10   ibid., p. 264.

11   James Gibb Stuart, *The Lemming Folk*, William MacLellan, Glasgow, 1980, pp. 132–33.

12   Guy Rais, 'Blunt's treachery "may have put lives of agents at risk"', *Daily Telegraph*, 3 March 1983.

13   id., No. 8, p. 280.

14   ibid.

15   *Sunday Times*, 4 October 1981.

16   In 1937 Krivitsky defected to the West. He identified one Soviet agent in the British Foreign Office, Captain John King, who was secretly tried and imprisoned. Additionally, he identified another, who turned out to be Donald Maclean; but no action was taken Lastly, he pointed out, but could not name, a British RIS agent who had been in Spain as a journalist – Philby.

17   Letter to the author from General Rich dated 1 March 1984.

18   Letter to the author from Kermit Roosevelt dated 28 November 1984.

19   They were SOE missions. The SOE recruited a variety of Communists, pro-Communists and left-wingers to the extent that the former SOE agent, Bickham Sweet-Escott, in his book, *Baker Street Irregular* (pp. 13–14) penned 'that SOE was a racket, peopled by wrong-headed and irresponsible young men, by embusqués or by crypto-communists, if not by out-and-out traitors'. The left included: James Eyre, Elliot Watrous, of whom Colonel McLean said 'He had very "progressive" views and we felt that he was supporting the Communist cause against the nationalists at every level' (*The Great Betrayal* by Lord Bethell, p. 16), and Reginald Hibbert who subsequently had an SIS/Foreign Service career At the end of the war the role of the SOE was taken over by British Special Operations (BSO). During the first post-war decade the BSO in the Eastern Mediterranean were 'virtually a wholly-owned subsidiary of the Soviets' doing 'dedicated work in arming the Greek Communists'. (*New Leader*, New York, 11 February 1985.)

20   In 1981, the former French Security Officer, Pierre de Villemarest, looked into the Klugman dossier and 'discovered that no Security inquiry into Klugman had been carried out despite the fact that he had been a SIS member for many years and although he was involved in several "affairs" at least one of which, in 1952, revealed him to have been a recruiting agent for Soviet intelligence in Oxbridge

193

circles. Klugman died in 1967 … Among Klugman's recruits were several future MPs, among them Bernard Floud whom PM Wilson considered including in his cabinet in 1967. Floud, an avowed Communist, entered the SIS and recruited in his turn several agents, only three or four of whom were discovered. One could name ten MPs like Floud.' Letter dated 10 February 1983.

21 Information to the author from a former OSS agent.
22 The greater part of the letter had been drafted by Bill Harvey, a friend of Philby.
23 Information to the author from Mrs Cook.
24 Patrick Seale and Mary McConville, *Philby, the Long Road to Moscow*, Hamish Hamilton, London, 1973, p. 251.
25 Information to the author from Miles Copeland.
26 E. H. Cookridge, *The Third Man*, Arthur Barker Limited, London, 1968, p. 252.
27 id., No. 18.
28 Wilbur Crane Eveland, *Ropes of Sand*, W. W. Norton & Company, New York, 1980, p. 320.
29 The source of information, for legal reasons, cannot be published.
30 *Morning Telegraph*, Sheffield, 15 May 1985.
31 ibid.
32 Information to the author from a former British Naval officer.
33 Letter to the author from George Kennedy Young, dated 11 March 1985.
34 id., No. 25.

13 Endgame

1 *Sunday Times*, 22 November 1987, p. 18.
2 *Time*, 30 November 1987, p. 9.
3 *EIR*, 27 November 1987, p. 55.
4 *Sunday Times*, 20 March 1988, p. 3.
5 *The Star*, 28 December 1987, p. 8.
6 'Greene and I – by Philby', *Daily Telegraph*, 18 January 1988, p. 1.
7 Information to the author from Chapman Pincher.
8 A report compiled by the Security and Intelligence Foundation [representing the CIA, FBI, NSA and DIA] published in *Nightwatch*, Vol. 3, No. 6, June 1988, Arlington, Virginia.
9 Information to the author from Miles Copeland.
10 'Traitor Philby is Dead at 76 in Moscow', *The Times*, 12 May 1988, p. 1.

11   ibid.
12   'Traitor Philby is Dead', *Daily Express*, 12 May 1988, p. 1.
13   Phillip Knightley, *Philby, KGB Masterspy*, Andre Deutsch, 1988, p. 262.

Appendix

1   *EIR* 31 March 1989, p. 33. See also 'The daughter of the "Fifth man": Who is Emma Rothschild really?', *EIR*, 29 September 1989, pp. 43–45.
2   Anthony Glees, *The Secrets of the Service*, Jonathan Cape, London, 1987, p. 413.
3   *Daily Telegraph*, 4 December 1986. What this 'unequivocal, evidence' is remains unknown. Some have suggested that it was: a) The information Rothschild gave to the Security Service on the Cambridge scientist Alister Watson in the early fifties; b) The information Flora Soloman had on Kim Philby (a friend, she suspected him of being a Communist and pro-Arab), passed by Rothschild to the authorities in late 1962.
       It is hard to believe that this would be sufficient to convince sceptical counter-intelligence officers. After all, the Soloman information was passed across several months after the government had had it confirmed that Philby was an RIS agent. Rothschild was too late to 'shop' Philby.
4   Indeed, the Security Service did not like the way Rothschild had forced them into such a reply.
5   *Daily Express*, 7 December 1986.
6   Nigel West, *Molehunt: the Full Story of the Soviet Spy in MI5*, Weidenfeld and Nicolson, London, 1987, p. 85. Through his solicitors Rothschild did issue a writ against West but later withdrew it deciding 'since the whole book is based on conjecture, there is nothing to warrant the issue of a writ'. (*Observer*, 22 March 1987.) Very generous, but Lord Rothschild does like to avoid the publicity a court case would no doubt bring. Indeed, he has always been quick to contact his lawyers. When in the mid-1960s Leitch, Page and Knightley were researching and writing their book about Philby, they received a letter from Rothschild's lawyers strongly demanding, for legal reasons, that Rothschild's name be not linked to those of Philby, Burgess and Maclean. He was not. Twenty years later, he is.
7   *Evening Standard*, 2 November 1979.

8   *Daily Express*, 3 March 1987.

9   E. H. Cookridge, *The Third Man*, Arthur Barker, London, 1968, pp. 12–13.

10 Cookridge, op. cit., pp. 114–115.

11 Boyle, op. cit., pp. 279–220.

12 *Sunday Times*, 3 April 1988.

13 Another proven recruiter was the Soviet scientist, Peter Kapitza, who was at Cambridge between 1921 and 1935, and, according to an SIS source 'was a Cheka agent'; he and Rothschild were 'great friends'. It is of interest to note that at that time, the scientific community in Cambridge was the first to be explored and targeted by the RIS. In November 1986, in Australia, Peter Wright made an 'in camera' statement about Kapitza and Rothschild which 'puzzled' Rothschild (Pincher, Web of Deception, p. 149). Special Branch officers then 'questioned him [Rothschild] about Peter Kapitza'. We understand that the Security Service were worried about this because Wright had made no mention in his files about Rothschild and Kapitza – had Wright been covering-up for his powerful mentor, 'Russophile' and 'fellow traveller'? (*Private Eye*, 4 September 1987, p. 25). Most interesting of all were the statements, again provided 'in camera', by Wright about Rothschild. Within weeks questions were asked in the House of Commons as to Rothschild having been a Soviet agent. What had Wright said? Certain counter-intelligence officers suspect that Rothschild had made a full 'confession' to Wright, which unlike Blunt's confession, he did not record upon file. One wonders what such a 'confession' would contain. In *Spycatcher* (p. 259) Wright reveals how 'Victor and Tess [his wife] were a constant help during the D3 [the Soviet counter-espionage branch's research unit] inquiries into the 1930s. Both knew so much about the personalities and the hidden relationships of the period, and were often able to prevail upon otherwise reluctant inhabitants of the Ring of Five's [Philby, Burgess, Maclean, Blunt and the First Man] menagerie to meet me. Victor was also able to make a number of vital introductions for me.' The next sentence implies that key information had been given to Wright by Rothschild: 'My suspicions fell on the renowned Soviet scientist Peter Kapitza ... [he] remained close to the Soviet government, and on several occasions was observed receiving Russian intelligence officers in his rooms... For years it was rumoured inside MI5 that Kapitza had talent-spotted potential recruits inside the Cavendish. But no one had ever really traced through the story... It

was just another loose end.' How convenient for someone close to Wright.

One can pose one very important question: how did Wright know that Kapitza had been observed receiving Russian intelligence officers in his rooms? We doubt that Special Branch officers would have been around. Had Rothschild been privy to Kapitza's espionage world and later confessed his 'involvement' to Wright? This former Security Service officer always 'protected' his mentor, Rothschild. When the Soviet defector Golitsyn pointed to Victor and Tessa Rothschild as being wartime RIS agents, he countered by charging that 'It sounded like KGB anti-Semitism'. (*Spycatcher*, p. 317.) Wright, for whatever his reasons, did not want to know.

14 *Sunday Express*, 3 April 1988.
15 Ted Allbeury, *The Other Side of Silence*, Granada, London, 1982, p. 85. Allbeury is a former SIS officer.
16 Information from a former SIS agent and Security Service conduit.
17 Letters (deposited with the Hoover Institute, California) 28, 30 and one undated, September 1963.
18 *Spycatcher*, p. 317.
19 Another RIS agent acquaintance of Rothschild was Rolf Katz, who 'advised that he met Burgess in England in 1936, when he, Katz, was assisting Lord Victor Rothschild'. (FBI interrogation report 14 July 1951. FBI FOIA files, Harry S. Truman Presidential Library.) '...Katz, within his extensive network of homosexual and Comintern contacts, also contributed to Rothschild's private intelligence network that, at the time, shared with Stalin a common enemy: Hitler.' (John Costello, *Mask of Treachery*, Collins, 1988, p. 305.)
20 In the mid-1930s Straight, as chairman of the Socialist Society, used his veto to stop Teresa Mayor joining the Communist movement. (Costello, *Mask of Treachery*, p. 266.) Rothschild's second wife, therefore, was a would-be Communist. Both Rothschild and Teresa were wartime Security Service officers.
21 *The Lobster*, No. 13, p. 3.
22 *Sunday Telegraph*, 16 April 1989, p. 3.

Book Reviews

1 Information to the author from Colonel 'Billy' McLean, 1984.
2 This humanitarian recruitment did not surprise the former SIS and Security Service officer, Anthony Cavendish: 'We [SIS] all did it.' Interview 1987.

3　Publication of the 1990 edition caused SIS to become stratospheric.
4　Information to the author from George Miller, 1983.
5　Information to the author from Anthony Samson, 1995. The case never went to court.
6　*Sunday Telegraph*, 16 April 1989, p. 3.
7　*Surveillant*, Washington, 1994, p. 1.
8　Except the present book, pp. 72–108.
9　Mandarin, *The Perfect English Spy*, Tom Bower, 1996, pp. 178–9.
10　*The Lobster*, Hull, No. 16.
11　Information to the author from Professor John Birks, Norway, early 1995.

Security Service (MI5) Input

1　Present address: PO Box 3255, Thames House, London, SW1P 1AE.
2　Information to the author from Major Fred Holroyd.
3　Ibid. For 20 years Holroyd has been fighting his case over false incarceration in Netley. Lord Trefgate, MOD, announced that medical information would be available for legal or medical advisers about Holroyd and Netley. Subsequent enquiries on behalf of Holroyd were met with the official reply: 'Medical records are not available.' So much for his Lordship's words.